VIJ

ALSO BY VIKRAM VIJ

Vij's Indian: Our Stories, Spices and Cherished Recipes

Vij's at Home—Relax, Honey:
The Warmth & Ease of Indian Cooking

Vij's: Elegant & Inspired Indian Cuisine

VIJ

**A CHEF'S ONE-WAY TICKET TO CANADA
WITH INDIAN SPICES IN HIS SUITCASE**

VIKRAM VIJ

with Nancy Macdonald

PENGUIN

an imprint of Penguin Canada, a division of Penguin Random House Canada Limited

Canada • USA • UK • Ireland • Australia • New Zealand • India • South Africa • China

First published 2017

www.penguinrandomhouse.ca

LIBRARY AND ARCHIVES CANADA CATALOGUING IN PUBLICATION

Vij, Vikram, author
Vij's: a chef's one-way ticket to Canada with Indian spices
in his suitcase / Vikram Vij.

ISBN 978-0-670-06950-7 (hardback)
ISBN 978-0-14-319421-7 (electronic)

1. Vij, Vikram. 2. Cooks—Canada—Biography.
3. Businessmen—Canada—Biography. I. Title.

TX649.V56A3 2017   641.5092   C2016-904748-2

Cover and interior design by Colin Jaworski
Cover image by Aaron Aubrey
Photo on page 144 by Tracey Kusiewicz | Foodie Photography
Photos on pages 160 and 224 by Aaron Aubrey
Photo on page 170 courtesy of the Canadian Broadcasting Corporation

Printed and bound in the United States of America

10 9 8 7 6 5 4 3 2 1

Penguin
Random House
PENGUIN CANADA

Strength does not come from physical capacity. It comes from an indomitable will.

—MAHATMA GANDHIJI

CONTENTS

VIJISMS

If you're going to fail, then fail loudly.

*

Cooking should be like sex—slightly different each time.

*

Use the animals from the guts to the nuts.

*

Use your hands to eat.
You don't make love with a knife and fork.

PREFACE

I am a sword. I am an alloy of India, of Austria, of Canada.

My culinary journey began in India, cooking with my aunts, and my mother, and my grandparents. I was forged in India. I was beaten and hardened by Austria. And sharpened and shaped by Canada.

When I opened my first restaurant, my father said to me: "Just give them butter chicken and tikka masala. White people can't tell the difference between one curry and another."

His advice, boiled down, was, "Serve it cheap. Label it 'ethnic.'" He saw no reason to shake up the model. Why change what's already working?

But I wasn't opening an Indian restaurant to make money. My mission was to bring awareness to the cooking and culture I had left behind. I wanted Indian cuisine to be given the same respect and love as French, as Italian. My goal, always, has been to elevate India's cooking and culture.

And this? Well, this is the story of how I did it.

Namaste.

—Vikram Vij, August 2016

Mama with Gauri and me, aged three and five, at an Amritsar street market in 1969.

AN INDIAN CHILDHOOD

I DIDN'T ALWAYS WANT TO BE A CHEF. But looking back, I believe it was my fate. From the start, all of my happiest memories involved food. Even as a boy I loved to cook. And to eat.

When guests would visit I would offer them tea, a sandwich. I loved the accolades, people clapping their hands, exclaiming, "Wow, what great chai!" Or, "You couldn't have made this biscuit!" I still love the praise. What a rush.

In India, you grow up fussing and obsessing over food because everyone around you is fussing and obsessing over food. To feed someone is an expression of love. Mama, Kusum is her name, spent hours in the kitchen, dicing vegetables, sweating over steaming curries tailored to my precise specifications. She didn't have to say "I love you." She did it every time she put a plate in front of me, the saffron rice spiked with peppers, just so.

I was always a chubby child. Even as a boy, when I was running wild, chasing my friends through the back lanes, playing cricket long after the sun set, I was a little fat. Mama, my grandmothers, my aunts, they were always treating me—orange cream biscuits after school, a little kheer after dinner—lavishing their affections by stuffing me with confections.

I believe my blue eyes were the reason I was showered with such love, such affection. In India, they're as rare as a white tiger—people used to stop my mother on the street to stare. I was as pampered as the village cow.

In India, food, of course, is also how you express your anger. And your power. When Bibiji, my grandmother Sarla, would announce to the table, "These onions have been sautéed a little too long," she was actually saying, "My cooking is superior to my daughter-in-law's. My daughter-in-law may be younger and more beautiful, but I'm still the better cook." She was empowering herself, showing her dominance. But we were all critics, not just Bibiji. My Papa, Manmohan, hated hot spices. He liked softer, more subtle flavours. I loved them.

When you grow up with those influences, food becomes a part of you. You barely finish your milky chai and think, What are we going to have now? As soon as your spoon hits the table your mind turns to the next snack, the next meal. It sparks an eternal competition: We were constantly pushing to improve the old recipes. We could always do better. This needs a bit more heat, I would think, or, Mama should have spiked the kheer with cinnamon.

But I digress. I'm getting ahead of myself.

I was born in 1964 in Amritsar, in the northwestern state of Punjab not far from the Pakistan border, and moved to Bombay when I was twelve. That was decades before the great, bustling metropolis was renamed Mumbai. I still stumble over the new name. My beloved Bombay will always be just that, never Mumbai.

In between, my family lived in Delhi. That's how Indians refer to New Delhi, the Indian capital. Calcutta, the old capital under the British Raj, is now known as Kolkata, which is closer to what the word sounds like in Bengali. But you'll never hear anyone refer to it as anything but Calcutta. We delight in confusing, I suppose.

For the first three years of my life, I didn't speak. Not a word. Not "Mama." Not "Papa." My grandmother was panicked: "I've got the most perfect little grandson," she'd tell her friends. "He runs, he jumps, he smiles. But he can't say a word."

"Relax," my mother would tell her. "He'll talk when he's ready." But my father, like his mother, was up in arms: "We can't have a son who doesn't speak!" he would shout. Eventually, Mama grew tired of fighting them. One morning, in tears, she allowed my grandmother take me to the doctor: Bibiji had convinced herself that it was a cleft issue, and wanted me to have surgery to allow my tongue freer movement. The doctor took one look and said, "He's perfectly fine. Some kids take to speaking a bit later than others. It doesn't mean a thing."

But it made sense. Our home was deathly quiet. My father liked it that way. He didn't like noise; he rarely spoke. This made my mother very reserved and quiet. To keep him contented, I sup-pose. I was the only child then; Gauri, my sister, was not yet born. So I didn't pick up the Hindi my parents spoke because there just wasn't a lot of it floating around me.

"Just you wait," the doctor told my mother. "The day he starts talking, he won't shut up." And that's exactly what happened. A month after my visit to the doctor, I started speaking, out of the blue. And once I started, I never stopped. I wake up talking. I go to sleep talking. I wake in the middle of the night and start talking to myself.

★

These days it's become fashionable to brag of humble roots. But I can't lay claim to a family of dusty subsistence farmers. We were not dabbawalas from a dank slum eking out a shantytown existence delivering tiffin meals to city workers. We were middle class— hardly genteel by North American standards, but in an era when most Indians grew up in shacks with mud floors, it set us apart.

I was born in an apartment. And by the time I was a school- boy we had a house. It was concrete, small and simple, built right smack in the centre of Delhi. Centipedes and house lizards scuttled up the walls. But it was ours. At the time, almost 60 percent of the population, more than a quarter of a billion people, were living in poverty.

It was all because of my father that we could lay claim to those four walls. Years earlier, he'd bought the plot of land on which it would be built. He believes in land: That you buy land. That you never rent. It's one of the lessons he imparted to me—or tried to. It is a rule I have been known to break. But more on that later.

Slowly, over the years, Papa erected a home on that plot, bit by bit. I remember visiting the work site with him on weekends so that he could make sure the contractor had erected the foundation as promised. We'd fill jerry cans with water to clean up the con- crete dust. I'd pile bits of scrap metal and push together tidy mounds of sawdust for Mama to sweep up. No one could afford a car then. She'd carry me there on the back of our scooter.

In 1971, when I was seven, we moved in.

This was his castle, but still Papa splurged on just one room: In the middle, he built a great big kitchen. It became the centre of our family life. At the back were two little bedrooms and a veranda.

Papa had a will of steel. The most important lesson he taught me was tenacity: No matter what happens, you keep your head down, you keep focused, you keep working toward your goal. The noise is just that. To this day, no matter what misfortunes might befall me—whether a project falls through or a business goes south—I put on a brave face, I push forward, I soldier on, I greet my guests with a wide smile at five-thirty p.m. when we throw open the restaurant's doors.

They'll have no idea I've just had to sell a building to make ends meet, or that I've been losing $50,000 a month on a factory I don't know how to turn around. I have my father to thank for that hard-boiled determination.

My sense of morality also came from him. Whatever I owe, I repay, down to the penny. Growing up, it used to bug the shit out of me when Papa would say, "Give me back my two rupees, twenty-five paisas." The exactness of his demand drove me up the wall. But as a businessman, I came to understand the importance of precision, of repaying your debts. That's how a reputation is earned, then cemented.

My father earned money, but he became wealthy by being frugal: From not going out to eat, from refusing to buy a new pair of pants, from denying himself a sweet for the long walk home from the train station. Truly, he's never known any of life's small pleasures. In this way he was his father's perfect opposite.

Roshan, his Papa and my grandfather, had been an extremely wealthy man. But as far as I remember, he never actually worked. Dadaji played cricket. He gambled. He drank. He was social, and a man of large appetites. But all his money had come from his father, who was a merchant, a landowner with a bustling jewellery shop. Family lore has it that at one point Papa's family owned half of

Amritsar. But by the time my father was a child, Dadaji had managed to piss it all away. He made bad business decisions. And the rest he lost playing rummy and flash. At the card tables, someone would float him a little cash in return for a tiny plot of land. He kept carving into the family holdings, parcelling them out piece by piece, sometimes betting big to try to cover off an earlier mistake. As much as he loved cards, Dadaji was no good at them. Eventually, that fortune was all gone. Poof. Just like that.

It left my father bitter. Anger courses through him like a forgotten kettle left to boil on a hot stove. He'd watched his father burn through the family fortune at a tender and meaningful age; as a child, it had forced him to face the terror of shifting fortunes.

As a teenager he'd had everything. He was driven to school in a car. He had horses. The family had a cook. Then suddenly, all that was taken from them. He had to learn to use a bicycle, a huge step down. He had to leave school at seventeen to try to earn a living.

He felt his youth had been taken away from him, that his father had squandered his future and respectability along with his own. In the end, he went to work for his mother's father.

That history made my father penny-wise, deeply prudent. He was going to hold on to every paisa he earned. And by and large he has.

My father would take out some of that frustration on my mom, on his staff, on me. The smallest thing could set him off. He'd totter around his shop like some tinpot raj, yelling orders. He kept his foot stamped hard on the throttle, always. He needed to dig his family out from under the mountain of shit that had been piled atop them.

But as hard as he pushed, I pushed right back. Our fights were legendary. He thought I was like a ball of naan dough, that he could mould me into the image of his making—push here, pull this a bit, roll out the lumpen bits. That I was his to remake in his image. He believed in shaping his bushes; but he didn't realize his son was a wild jungle.

We used to have raging fights over the most inconsequential things. He wanted me to have short hair. Why? Because "real men" have short hair. It was the 70s. I loved my long, wavy dark hair. He would point to examples: "Nelson Mandela has short hair." And "Gandhiji had short hair." Great people, I would admit, but not because of their hair.

Our stubbornness is equally matched, and these fights could rage for days as my mother begged me to back down. Like Gandhi, I would go on a hunger strike, my own private act of civil disobedience, until Papa relented and let me keep my hair.

Even today I keep my hair long and curly. And every time he sees me the first thing he'll say is, "My God, you need a haircut." In some ways I'm still his impish son, challenging him. But it's funny. As hard as I fight it, I am so like him. My temper can be explosive. I can lose it completely the way I remember he could. It is an affliction.

From the start, I was my own man. I loved Papa, and I probably relied on him long after I should have. But I've always known who held the keys to my destiny. It wasn't him.

I am like my grandfather, whom I adored. I love to spend. If I bring in $100, I'll go out and spend $110. Then I'll run around like a madman trying to cover it. That's the story of my life. When we were kids, Papa thought that by giving my sister and me pocket money he would teach us frugality, budgeting, and impulse control. I learned none of that. I would rush out to treat myself to a Tutti Frutti ice cream bar—always pistachio with saffron nut. By the afternoon I'd be borrowing from Gauri because I'd blown through all my money and had nothing left for the rest of the week. I was always in the hole, trying to repay her.

I remember my grandmother cupping my hands together one day: If water drips through, it means you will never lose money. But if water escapes, it means money will, too. My palms, well, they've always been like colanders.

The men in my family are all reactionary. It's as if we grew up silently promising not to become our fathers. Dadaji was a spend-thrift, determined to enjoy life the way he never saw his hard-working father enjoy his. I'm just like him: I grew up watching my father pinch pennies, cut corners. It's like I want to make up for it—to enjoy life for us both.

To this day he'll never spend a cent. He wears thirty-year-old pants. He'll soak a tea bag twice. But you have to give it to Papa: his immense drive, his business savvy. By the time I was born, he wasn't yet thirty but had a shop of his own and a small textiles empire in the making.

Mama was softer, shy, uncomplicated. She made sure Gauri and I were properly fed and bathed, that our schoolwork was done. She loved me deeply, unconditionally. She always believed that her handsome, blue-eyed boy would bring great pride to the Vij family.

She was in my corner, sneaking an extra egg into my ome-lettes, treating me to bhelpuri, a snack made from puffed rice and tangy tamarind sauce after Papa had lit into me. And she protected me. If I'd failed an exam or got into a scuffle at school, I knew I could go to her. "Let's wait for a better time to tell Papa," she'd say, trying to keep the peace. She'd keep the bad news from him until his mood lifted. She'd mollify my teachers, too: "No, no—don't worry. He's just a little bit naughty," she'd say, apologizing for whatever new disruption I'd caused. When we got home she'd light into me, though I never took her seriously. It went in one ear and out the other. Poor Mama.

Mama was very elegant. She loved to dress up, to put on new saris, to load up her arms with bangles, to go out. My father hated all that. It was expensive, unnecessary. He'd stop her from applying makeup, from treating herself to a particularly exquisite bindi. "What is the point?" he'd ask. "We have perfectly good food at home. We can play music on the radio." She always deferred to him. She never once pushed back. She never sulked. She never complained. But over the years, I watched as some of her passion wilted. I sometimes think part of her died after she married.

Papa never laid a finger on her. Not once. But he was such a frustrated person—by his father's drinking, by circumstance. I think my mother bore more than her share of his frustration, his quiet rage.

Her tactic was to shut up, to endure. Over the years she learned to listen to him with one ear. But you'll never once hear her complain. She adores my father.

★

Mama was one of nine: five boys and four girls. Her father came from a line of silver merchants from Andaman, which is part of the remote Nicobar and Andaman island chain in the Bay of Bengal, closer to Burma, really, than to India. But it was close to the Indian imagination, thanks to Andaman's infamous colonial prison, Kala Pani, or "Black Waters"; it was named for the dark ocean that surrounded it. British authorities had exiled political prisoners to the dreaded penal colony. It was India's Alcatraz, its Robben Island, and teemed with bugs and scorpions. Freedom fighters, held in solitary, were tortured. Some chose suicide over a stay at Kala Pani.

Mama's father's family built up a trade in silver on the Andaman and Nicobar chain. After partition, the family moved to Delhi, then the brand-new capital. Even under the British Raj, Delhi had remained the political and financial centre.

Mama's parents, Chaiji and Bauji, as I knew them, were lovely. They spoiled me terribly. My Chaiji was pretty, and a bit chunky. (I come by it honestly, I guess. We're all a bit fat.) On Saturdays, I would wake early to visit them. I'd catch the seven-thirty bus. Bauji, my grandfather, would meet me, waiting for me at their stop, to take my hand. Together, we'd take a rickshaw to the market to shop.

Everyone doted on me. Mama's brothers would mock Papa behind his back: "Look at your stupid father—you'll never amount to anything," they'd tease. "What's wrong with your teeth?" my aunts would ask when I'd lost a tooth. "Too much sugar," they'd giggle, wagging their fingers in my face. They didn't mean a word of it. That's what Indian families do: We make fun, we taunt one another. My long wavy hair was an endless source of amusement to them all.

My aunts would pay me one rupee to perform little plays, like their little circus boy. My father was furious when he found out. He sat them down and told them not to dote on me, not to indulge me. He wanted me to be intelligent, to get ahead through hard work. And he felt they were pushing me to become an actor.

In reality, no one was pressuring me. I didn't need any encouragement. I adored acting. Performing, even more than food, was my first love.

From time to time, I used to dress as a woman. I would put on Mama's spiky heels, her sandals dyed hot purple. I'd don her pink sari and feather boas and stick a red bindi between my eyes. I would deftly apply lipstick and line my eyes with kohl, my arms with thin bangles, and jangle around the house pretending to be a woman.

It's not that I was trans: I just loved acting. I loved drama, improvisation, being on stage—all of it. I always thought I was going to be an actor. When I was twelve I won the school's drama competition for acting in a one-man play where I played a ghost, surely the only school award I ever won.

The kitchen was simply a more acceptable stage—a way to explore my creativity, once I'd realized that Papa would never allow me to try my luck in Bollywood. But more on that later.

The only time Mama ever got really mad at me was in 1976. A few years earlier, she and my father had taken a trip to Europe together. I remember the incident like it was yesterday. They'd brought home a pellet gun for a cousin. I kicked up a huge fuss. I desperately wanted that gun. I "needed" that gun, I told them. I fought my cousin for ownership. I would grab it from him, fill it with pellets, and shoot targets: lizards—they're like bugs in India; they're everywhere—and sometimes, though I'm ashamed to admit it, small birds.

I was a little bully with that rifle. I loved the weight of it in my hands, the attention it got me, inflating my too-healthy ego. I had a good eye and a steady shot. Neighbourhood kids would flock to watch me shoot. I would saunter around like a little dictator. I'd taken to wearing a red bandana.

One day, I was playing with friends. The son of my father's good friend ran past, dribbling a football. "Give me that ball," I said.

"No—I'm playing with it," he said.

"Give it to me or I'll shoot you," I replied.

When he grabbed the ball and turned to run, I aimed the gun at his back and pulled the trigger. It was, without question, the ugliest thing I have ever done. The second I did it, the realization flooded through me and I dropped to my knees.

"Are you okay?" The words tumbled from my mouth in a panicked stream. "Did I hurt you?" I was appalled with myself: I had shot a boy.

I was twelve years old. Morally, I knew it was dead wrong, but I also knew there could be legal repercussions. So I was shit-scared, too. I rushed home and climbed into bed, too stricken, too scared to move. Suddenly, I heard a crush of people outside the house: the boy, his mother, and what seemed like half the neighbourhood crowded in behind them—for support, or something to do.

"Look what a bully your son is!" the boy's mother shrieked. "Look what he's done to my baby!" she said, lifting his red T-shirt, revealing an ugly—but certainly not life-threatening—wound.

Mama was horrified when she heard what had happened. She'd never seen that side of me. Even worse, the boy was the son of my father's friend.

Somehow, Mama managed to calm the boy's mother. She dragged me from my room and forced me to apologize.

"I'm sorry," I said. "I didn't mean to hurt you." But then I tried to argue—as though it was his fault, that he should have handed over the ball. The shouting started all over again, and a melee broke out anew in the living room.

"You are dead wrong," Mama said through gritted teeth. "Get to your room."

I was in bed when they finally left. Mama came tearing in. I'd never seen her so angry in my entire life—not before, and certainly never since. She lifted me out of bed and took out her leather belt. She was furious. But even more, she was terrified by what could have been. I could have been hauled off by the corrupt local police. I could have been beaten by that angry mob.

Mama, the world's biggest softie, completely lost it on me, slapping at my hands, screaming at me. Then she told Papa, as soon as he returned, so I took another beating. Being slapped or having my arm twisted was nothing new to me. But my mother had never gone there with me before. Even today, if Mama gets a little mad when I haven't called or visited, I feel deeply and immediately ashamed. I still remember how livid she was. I never want to feel that anger and burning shame from her again.

The gun was taken from me forever. No matter how much I begged for it, I was never allowed to fire it again. Nor even to touch it without permission. It sat rusting on a shelf. I'd beg to clean it, just to feel it again. Then I'd brush off the rust, oil and shine it, then carefully wrap it in paper and replace it on the shelf. It's still in Bombay somewhere, rotting away. I've asked my father a couple of times to bring it to me, but he always says the same thing he did then: "You don't deserve it."

But something else came of that European trip, beyond the gun. For my father, it represented yet another disappointment. You see, Papa had always had a vision, a plan to escape India for London, where he planned to make a name for himself. That three-month holiday in Europe was actually a means to scope out the city, to see whether he could make a go of it there. He came home deeply in love—with the city, its pace, with the potential. He was desperate to emigrate. But Mama refused to go. She was unwilling to leave her family and all she knew. He fought and fought and fought her, to no avail. Mama refused to budge.

He used to supply cloth to a very dear friend in London, who became unbelievably wealthy selling saris and kurtas to second-generation Indians in Southall. "Look at Suresh—look how rich he's become," Papa would comment. What he was really saying was: "Look what could have become of us. Look what I could have achieved."

★

I worshipped Dadaji. Just as he loved me, and his scotch. At night, my grandfather would sit me in his lap and drink a few fingers of it, sometimes more. "I want you to open a restaurant, beta," he'd say, using the Hindi term of endearment for "son" or "boy." "You love to eat, and I love to drink." He would be the bartender in the restaurant of our dreams. There, his grandson wouldn't dare charge him for drinks. I would be the executive chef, and cook for us both. Decades later, I would name my restaurant Vij's in his honour, a nod to our shared dream.

Some of my happiest childhood memories are of Dadaji gripping my hand as we shopped at the markets on Lawrence Road in Amritsar. In Vancouver, it's become trendy to spend a lazy Sunday afternoon at the farmers' market. In India, you visit twice a day: once in the morning, then again in the evening. It's a way to get out of the house, to keep the kitchen running. At the time, men went to the markets and women stayed home to cook. Sometimes, Papa would go on the way to work. But on weekends my Dadaji and I would go together, on the rickshaw, to buy fruits, vegetables, spices. I loved the drama, the sights, the smells: mound after mound of tiny tindora cucumbers, deep green kerala, sweet-smelling watermelons piled beside bushels of fresh mint that cut the air with its crisp, sharp smell.

The streets outside were always thick with smoke: Street cleaners, who came from the lowest caste—mostly Dalits, also known as Untouchables—would amass cow dung and rubbish in great piles and burn it on the sidewalk (at the time in India, no one bothered to collect garbage). Brahmins would cross the street to avoid them; if even the shadow of a Dalit touched them, they would be forced to go home to shower, to cleanse themselves.

In the markets, the produce was spread on burlap mats—not oiled and stacked in geometric shapes, as in grocery stores. Often, the markets were as filthy as they were disorganized, especially after the monsoons, when everything was caked in mud. Near the butchers, we'd have to hop small rivers of blood. The smell of chickens would hit you like a gut punch, cutting through even the thick clouds of diesel, the rotten stench rising from open sewers.

And the noise, my God: the howling mutts, begging for scraps; the thwacking of heavy knives against butcher's blocks; the clucking chickens rattling their tinny cages; the honking of horns; the rickshaw drivers fighting over passengers; the sellers competing for customers. A true Indian bazaar. It was absolute "mela"—chaos.

"No seeds! No seeds!" the grape seller would yell when you drew near.

"My potatoes are the most delicious potatoes," the potato dealer would whisper conspiratorially. The cacophony of sound made it impossible to think. Dadaji would encourage it, pitting two onion sellers against each other, trying to strike a bargain.

"My onions are better than your onions," one would shout.

"That's not decent onion, man," Dadaji would say. "Come on!"

His competitor, squatting on his haunches, would needle in, pointing to the flaws—entirely imagined—of his neighbour's fare. Then he'd offer to cut the cost for a kilo by a third, but only for my grandfather.

And on it would go. Sellers would mock, undercut, and harass each other until the sun set. Then everyone would hang out and forget about the fighting, smoking together and chewing betel nut. It was just stupid drama, all part of the game.

On slow days, Dadaji would take me aside to teach me to judge quality. That's how I learned how to haggle, how to cut a better deal, how to select the ripest and tastiest vegetables. To this day, I still adore negotiating. Recently, I talked a manager at Whole Foods into a 25 percent discount for a pound of bruised tomatoes. I didn't care about saving money; I just love the fun, the rush of haggling a better deal.

Firm fruits like apples and pears should feel unyielding, but peaches, plums, and other supple, fleshed fruits should feel slightly soft. A hard fruit means it was picked too early and will go mealy as it ripens. My grandfather showed me to hunt for bruises that suggest it was roughly handled. Produce, when handled carefully, can produce extraordinary results.

For okra, look for a smooth texture with round edges. Toss those with hairy skin or rough ridges. A quick, neat break means the okra is fresh, while a soft and rubbery one suggests that it's stale.

My grandfather taught me early on that a tomato's taste can be gauged by running your fingers, ever so gently, over its smooth body. He taught me to choose deeply coloured tomatoes that are firm, with a little give, and have no wrinkles—a sure sign of age, as with people. "Smell them," he would tell me. Fruit beginning to spoil takes on a slightly sour odour. He'd cackle, delighted, when I learned my lesson.

★

My parents sent me to Summerfields, a decent English-medium private school in Kailash Colony, in south Delhi. No one who can afford private education sends their children to state schools. They're dreadful. Even today, more than 60 percent of Indian schoolchildren are privately educated.

Summerfields was a forty-five-minute walk from home. That walk was the best part of my day. The rest I'd spend being hauled out of the classroom by my left ear, smacked with a bamboo switch, and publicly admonished.

I was the class clown, the naughty one, always cracking jokes behind my poor teachers' backs, pushing boundaries, testing the limits of their patience.

Summerfields was intense. As a student, you were always on edge. Students were grouped into houses, like a proper British school, but these were named after Indian greats: Gandhi, Tagore, Nehru. Each house had wardens to enforce discipline during assembly and break time.

The premise was to raise little gentlemen, with a premium placed on self-discipline, helpfulness, and thoroughness. My light blue shorts had to be kept impeccably clean. Even our fingernails were monitored for cleanliness. In this environment, I was hopeless.

At the time, I felt really bad about my dreadful marks. I'm so stupid, I can't retain a thing, I used to think. I felt my eyes had cursed me, and secretly hated them: God, why did you give me these eyes—why didn't you give me brains instead? I would have been so much better off born smart, I thought.

Every teacher I had labelled me "disruptive." It hurt so much. But not anymore. Today I know beyond a shadow of a doubt that being disruptive and shaking up the usual method is crucial to entrepreneurship. You cannot succeed in the restaurant industry or in business if you're not innovating, if you're not finding a new way, if you're not challenging the status quo. Too many are crushed by their experiences at school. I almost was.

Summerfields may have been leagues above what a government school looked like, but we were still being taught in tents. India was still very poor. Only in the upper forms did you learn in proper outbuildings. The canvas classrooms for primary students were like ovens, with temperatures routinely running into the forties, compounding my inability to stay awake. Some had a single standing fan in a corner—as laws required—chugging away at a quarter speed.

It was there, in the heat of the afternoon, papers curling in the humidity, that my mind would wander: back to a beamer I'd bowled the night before during a game of gully cricket, to the *Champak* comic book I'd been reading that morning—anywhere but the day's lesson. Some days, I might as well have not been there at all.

My marks, unsurprisingly, were not pretty. "He's always dreaming, thinking of something else," the teachers would rightly explain. "Every time I turn my back he's cracking a joke, disrupting the class." One of my tricks was to hum in a low monotone, "hmmmmmmmmmmm." There were dozens and dozens of us in the tent, and my poor teachers could never make out which of us was playing the fool. "Who's making that noise?" they would shout, cracking up my classmates, encouraging me. "Stop that humming!"

To try to offset some of my father's ire at my misbehaviour, I would try to feign a medical excuse: "I can't hear the teachers," I would tell my parents. Or "I can't read the blackboard." When it came to her first-born, her darling boy, my mother's well of patience had no bottom. Straight-faced, she would march me to a series of experts for a round of testing.

"He hears perfectly," the audiologist shrugged. "His vision is slightly better than 20/20," two separate optometrists told her. Mama would gently beg me to do better, to try harder, to stop playing the fool.

Upon seeing my report card my father would fly into a boiling rage. Afterward, he would settle into a dark, silent mood that could last weeks. To his credit, he never gave up on me. He kept pushing, trying to keep me on the right path, no matter how hard I tried to stray from it. It must have been so disheartening for my father—to struggle, to work so hard, to pay my outrageous school fees, and then to see me taking it all so lightly. "Just study!" he'd shout.

But I couldn't. I've since taught myself to sit still, but it's taken me years. When I work, I often pace, up and down. I jump from one thing to the next.

Papa thought my behaviour was the fault of my best friends: two neighbourhood boys, brothers, Anil and Sunil Monga. He wasn't entirely wrong. They were bad influences. Anil and Sunil were older than I was, and naughty as hell. I worshipped them. I suppose I was charismatic enough, or maybe just daring enough, that they would allow me to tag along with them. I worked hard to impress them. We often fought or wrestled, or played really physical games, like seven stones—the Indian version of dodgeball, but rougher. I loved it.

By the time I turned twelve, I had a girlfriend, Sonia Sarovar. My God, I loved her. That the feeling was rarely reciprocated made me all the more crazy for her. She was so beautiful, with pale, creamy skin and light brown eyes. But she knew she was gorgeous, and that made her more than a little mean.

Sonia lived across the street from us. She loved playing house, so of course I indulged her. I'd do anything she asked. She played the mom, I was the dad, and we had a young son: her younger brother. Gauri, my sister, younger by two years, had no interest in playing with us.

There are no two more different people in this world than Gauri and I: She is brilliant. A goody two-shoes. For her, school was a breeze. She rarely needed to study, and always brought home excellent marks. Her teachers adored her without exception. Papa never had to fight to convince her principals to take her in the way he did with me.

She is also the worst cook who has ever graced the earth. If she tried to put a pot of water on the stove she'd bloody burn it. I was supposed to be the lawyer, the engineer. She was supposed to learn to cook, to be the perfect housewife. It was the other way around: I became a chef, I loved to cook. She became a teacher. (She thinks it's hilarious that in the past two years I have received two honorary Ph.D.'s—the boy who never studied, now a doctor of laws!) Growing up, we fought like crazy, but I love her dearly.

Sometimes Sonia would let me kiss her, or we would make out.

It turned out that Anil and Sunil had crushes on Sonia too, though they knew nothing of our relationship, which Sonia kept secret. "I absolutely love her," one of them would prattle on. I never told them a thing about our relationship. I was convinced that one day I would marry her. I didn't want to jinx it.

★

Then, one spring day in 1977, when I was in seventh standard, Papa announced, out of the blue, that we were moving to Bombay. I would start eighth standard at a new school. I was devastated. All I could think was, "I can't leave Sonia." But Sonia was herself grieving: Her father had died suddenly, from heart failure. And she wasn't really interested in me—not that I could see it at the time.

It was a business decision. A few years earlier, Papa's textile business in Delhi had plateaued, and was beginning a gentle decline. The government was still a few years from launching its liberal economic reforms, and the local economy was stagnant. Worried, Papa had travelled alone to Bombay for three months; he'd scouted the Mulji Jetha Market, the huge bazaar in central Bombay that sold everything from unbleached muslin to fine silks and embroidered wedding saris. Papa was a semi-wholesaler, and his uncles helped him launch a store, which he named for them, according to the tradition of the era.

Bombay at the time was undergoing massive expansion and growth. The polychromatic city, port of arrival for millions of migrants, is a melting pot of different cultures, races, and social classes. Its then-population of just under nine million made it second in size only to Calcutta, but it had far more wealth than the old capital had seen in decades. It was—and still is—India's New York. Businesspeople, entrepreneurs, villagers who didn't want to live the way their parents had—anyone with chutzpah or a dream to break with destiny, and the lowly status afforded by caste, was gravitating to it.

Papa returned to Delhi, his mind made up: We were moving. He'd come home to pack us up. My mom didn't really factor into the decision. Nor did she oppose it. Her parents were in Delhi. But the subcontinent is embroidered with tens of thousands of kilometres of train tracks. The thirteen hundred–kilometre train trip, the rough equivalent of Montreal to Halifax, meant they could still visit, though not as frequently. Papa got me into a new school, the G.D. Somani School, in Cuffe Parade, which was then a brand-new neighbourhood at Bombay's southernmost point.

Long before it was a city, Bombay was a chain of seven islands off India's western coast. Gradually, reclamation and landfill united the landmass into single long island, like Manhattan. Cuffe Parade, at the far end of the chain, was the last neighbourhood to be developed. G.D. Somani was among its newest schools. They needed students. I'm sure that's how I got in.

But at the end of term, I managed to dampen the excitement of the move with news that I'd failed math at Summerfields. I would have to come back in July to rewrite my exam. Papa freaked out; he was appalled by this new low. But he was so preoccupied with the move to Bombay, with getting me into a new school and closing his business in Delhi, that I escaped the worst of it.

When we made it to Bombay, I had to sit down with my new principal, Master Tucker. "You seem like a bright boy," he said. "I need you to hit 60 percent in math, otherwise I'm going to have to ask you to leave the school." That meant transferring to a school three and a half kilometres away. For me, this was motivation enough. For the first and only time, I lived a block and a half from school.

For the next six months, I studied my ass off, night after night.

In the end, it worked: I scored far better than the marks I needed. Papa was thrilled, of course. But more importantly, it instilled a bit of confidence in me. That was intoxicating. That first term at G.D. Somani changed me forever.

I was never the brightest boy in the class. But my grades ceased being an unending familial concern. From then on, I was a middle-of-the-pack student. If there were sixty in our class, I would end up thirtieth, thirty-first, thirty-second from the top. I was hopeless in English, geography, and history, but I had a logical mind. Numbers made sense to me. Math, physics, and chemistry became my favourite subjects.

On the girl front, however, I was not so lucky. For the first few months I wrote to Sonia. "I miss you so much," I'd write. Pathetic little postcards expressing my undying love. At the time, it took weeks for her replies to reach me. I would have written twice or three times before receiving even a single note. Sonia's enthusiasm for me quickly waned. When I told her I'd go to Delhi to see her, I heard, through a cousin, that she didn't want me to come. I was heartbroken. I wanted to hold her again in my arms, to kiss her. But she wanted nothing to do with me. "Let's move on" came her eventual reply. Later, I learned she'd grown close to Anil and Sunil. That broke my heart.

That's the hair Papa and I fought so often over. Papa preferred a tight, military cut. There was no way I was going to lose those curls!

"NO SON OF MINE IS
BECOMING AN ACTOR"

AFTER COMPLETING MY MATRIC EXAMS, following tenth standard—
the last hurdle before graduation—I entered Bombay's Elphinstone
College. With its spires and turrets, the old school, built in the
Gothic revival style, looks like Eton, but in downtown Bombay.
After twelfth standard, I stayed on at Elphinstone to study chem-
istry. I was working on a Bachelor of Sciences degree.

That's when I met Shilka: impossibly cool, cosmopolitan, and
the most beautiful woman I'd ever seen. She was a smoker, an incredibly rebellious statement for an Indian woman at the time. She could
have been beaten for it. To me, it signalled that she was bold, fearless,
edgy. And though I hated the smell, I soon started smoking too.
Somehow, I thought the gesture was romantic. Long after Shilka,
the habit survived. I have never been addicted but I do love to smoke
socially, though I'll never have more than two or three in a day.

I couldn't believe it when Shilka asked me out. She was like a
drug: I couldn't get enough.

But Elphinstone, or academia generally, wasn't much for me. I wanted to perform, to be on a stage. By then, Papa had nipped my Bollywood dreams in the bud: "No son of mine is becoming an actor," he'd said. So I went looking for another creative outlet, one that Papa might consider respectable. I had no interest in following him into fabrics.

At the time, my cousin Niksu, my father's sister's son, was in Bad Hofgastein, Austria, studying at the School of Hotel Management. Growing up, I'd thought hotel life was so glamorous: the elegant women in their bright silk saris, the men in three-piece suits, the French cuisine, the dancing, the precision, the drama, the colour. I'd go to the Oberoi on Nariman Point, Bombay's main promenade, or to the ornate old Taj Hotel, or to the Hotel President, its white marble floors so clean you could practically see your reflection.

There, bellmen in towering red turbans would yank open the twin doors wide to allow me to enter, like a young Maharajah. I'd ride the elevator to the top floor, pretending that my parents had the penthouse, the air conditioning a brief reprieve from the cloying heat. It felt like a dream. Almost nothing else in India was air-conditioned at the time. I wore my best pants, a freshly pressed shirt, and Indian sandals. I made sure my feet were impeccably clean. I did it for years, making sure never to visit any one hotel so often that I might be recognized.

These were among India's dozen-odd five-star hotels with decent water pressure and modern plumbing, Western comforts out of reach of almost everyone in the country at the time. (One night at the Oberoi was equivalent to six months' wages for the average Indian.) Many of the new hotels sprouted up during Indira

Gandhi's reign to lure foreign tourists, exchange, and business. But the attraction wasn't limited to foreigners. I was also enchanted.

Even then, I was social and outgoing. I loved talking to people on the street, greeting relatives when they came to visit, offering sweet chai and homemade snacks. If Bollywood was out, then to me, the dream of working in this burgeoning industry felt like the next best thing.

That notion remains: I sometimes feel that at five-thirty, when the curtain draws and the doors open at Vij's for the night, I'm performing: welcoming my guests, inviting them in, shaking their hands, dancing across the room with a tray of fresh chutneys. My kitchen staff is in the back, choreographing the beautiful song and dance.

Papa loved the idea of me studying abroad. You see, my dream, in many ways, was also my father's. He'd always wanted to leave India, but circumstances had never allowed it. So when I brought up the idea of studying hotel management in Austria, tentatively at first, he jumped.

"Beta, you must go," he urged, immediately, forcefully. My application was quickly accepted. Chefs then were not the super-stars they are today. Culinary and hospitality schools were not being flooded with applicants.

The political situation hastened my departure: 1984 was marked by factional violence, terrorist acts carried out in the name of religion, and, in the end, mass murder. It remains one of the darkest years in modern Indian history.

For years, Sikhs had been advocating for "Khalistan," a separate Sikh state to be carved from the Punjab, the northern state of my birth. In and around Amritsar, where I'd grown up and where my extended family still lived, roaming gangs were beating and killing Hindus who opposed Khalistan. My Punjab had grown unsafe.

It was unclear where the instability might lead. In Amritsar, as Hindus, we were the minority religion. Papa was afraid for me. And he'd grown embittered by the violence. He didn't see a future for an India divided by religion. He felt I must leave.

It got worse when, in June, Prime Minister Gandhi ordered an attack on the Golden Temple in Amritsar, Sikhism's most sacred shrine. She did it to remove Jarnail Singh Bhindranwale, the militant Sikh leader who'd taken sanctuary on temple grounds, bringing a stockpile of weapons along with him. With the help of hundreds of followers, Bhindranwale had managed to turn the complex into a virtual military fortress. It was ultimately seized by the army. The bloody, controversial operation, code-named Blue Star, left thousands dead.

A month after I left, Gandhi was assassinated by two Sikh bodyguards, triggering a wave of killings. Frenzied mobs, hungry for revenge, burned Sikh-owned businesses, dragged Sikhs from their homes, from cars and trains, clubbing them to death or setting them aflame. Gandhi's murder triggered a counter-insurgency aimed at supporters of Khalistan. Constitutional rights were suspended in the Punjab, where the government carried out gross human rights abuses against tens of thousands of people. Some of my friendships with Sikhs fell apart because of it. I could no longer visit gurdwaras, their places of worship. As a Hindu, they were now closed to me. The situation has since changed dramatically. Punjab is again a peaceful state. *Wahe guru*—thank God.

I was in Austria by then. I'd made it out weeks before Gandhi was shot dead in the garden of the prime minister's residence.

"I am alive today, I may not be there tomorrow," she'd said a day before her assassination, an eerily prophetic final address, in Orissa. "I shall continue to serve until my last breath and when I die, I can say, that every drop of my blood will invigorate India and strengthen it."

It was then that I broke with religion and became the staunch atheist I am today. In my mind, an atrocity carried out in the name of God will always be wrong, just as I believe that an India splintered along religious lines can never succeed.

★

Moving money out of socialist India to pay for my studies in Europe was not easy. We had a distant relative in London, a vice-president of a multinational firm, who agreed to help. The money would be routed through him: He would arrange to pay my tuition fees from the U.K.

But there was only one way to get the money to him: hawalas, the trust-based money transfer systems that move funds across borders. Bombay's hawalas were clustered in Kalbadevi, the old trading district not far from the MJ Market where my father had his shop. I remember Papa taking me there after school.

After going up a flight of stairs and down a dingy hallway, we entered a dank little office, its interior lit by a single bulb. The broker had a tiny little desk, a few sheets of recycled paper, a pencil, and a telephone. With that, he could transfer money anywhere in the world, no questions asked, no names used, no paper trail for police to follow. You'd never see a woman in his shop: In India, money was still the sole preserve of men.

Hawalas like his were illegal, so at first, the trader denied the true nature of his business: "No, no. You've come to the wrong place," he said, practically shoving Papa and me out the door. Typically, traders dealt with trusted clients; he was scared we were cops, or informants. Papa and I returned numerous times until we became familiar to him.

The system involved nothing more than a code word and a handshake. A record was scribbled on a tiny slip, then destroyed when the deal was completed. Papa didn't have to provide his name, or that of our London relative. The code word was all my relative needed to pick up the cash—minus a commission—at the other end. But this was no Western Union. There were no guarantees. We were nervous, and with good reason, as it turned out.

It's an ancient system, and long predates Western banks. Arab traders used it to avoid robbery along the Silk Road, which is the reason for the name: *hawala* is Arabic for "trust." And the hawala broker proved to be far more trustworthy than our high-flying relative, who pocketed Papa's money, claiming he'd never received it.

The man was distantly related to Mama, but my father couldn't push her to ask after the money. For starters, women in India did not speak up at the time. And to challenge a senior, deeply revered member of the family, especially to accuse him of theft, was unthinkable.

"Leave it alone," my father said. "Just drop it."

Our deferential culture would protect my relative, and he knew it. We kept quiet. He kept our money.

In all, Papa lost fifty thousand rupees, the equivalent of roughly a thousand Canadian dollars. But to an Indian at the time, it would have felt more like fifty thousand dollars. It broke my heart.

"It's just money," Papa said, comforting me. But he was stricken. Papa had always prided himself on how careful and astute he was with money. He'd been tricked. But he put on a brave face.

"All I want is for my son to go to Austria. We'll find a way, beta," he promised.

My father has always had a big heart. There was nothing to do but earn the money back and send it again, he said. But time was against us. We couldn't wait, so he borrowed the money against his store, and we went back to the hawala. This time, it was routed to Niksu, my cousin in Bad Hofgastein, who was to pay my fees. Fifteen years later we heard that our London relation had been fired from his job for embezzling money.

Niksu, who knew none of this back story, was extremely blasé about his crucial role as middleman. We had to chase after him to make sure he'd received the money and paid my tuition fees. I'd write, then never hear back.

In those days, calling overseas was a nightmare. It took four years to process the permit for a home line. Papa refused to pay the bribe that might have sped things up. Even those lucky enough to have a home telephone could not dial internationally. I had to go to the Public Call Office, or the PCO, as it was known. The red and yellow booths were in every neighbourhood. You'd take a chit, then sit down on a plastic bench and wait, often for hours, for your turn.

Labour was cheap, and the three red phones were each manned by clerks. They'd ask where you were calling, then ask you to write out the number. After dialing, they would hand you the receiver. Like so much else in India at the time, the system's inefficiencies rendered it almost useless.

There were no phones in Niksu's dorm, so I would try to time the call to a small window—between afternoon class and dinner— when Niksu could receive calls in the school office. But if the line at the PCO was short, or the queue had advanced too quickly, my call would reach Austria too early: Niksu would still be in class. So I'd turn around and go to the back of the line, waiting for a second turn at the phones. By then, a group of migrant workers keen to phone home would inevitably have joined the queue, and by the time I got through to Austria, Niksu would have left for dinner.

In the end, by some small miracle, it all worked out. After repeated delays, my cousin arranged for my fees to be paid, and I got the green light to book my plane ticket.

But before I could fly out, there was one final hurdle I needed to clear: Foreign students were required to study German, and sit for a language exam before entry. So off I went to Pune, home of the nearest Goethe-Institut, to take a three-month crash course.

The Goethe-Institut, a cultural arm of the German government, taught free German-language classes throughout the world. Pune's was one of 150 erected in the decades after the Second World War to project a new German image to the world. In India, they're known as "Max Müller bhavans" to honour the German linguist and champion of all things Indian. Hindi and German, I came to learn, were— as Müller had discovered—remarkably similar languages.

Rather than returning to Bombay after sitting for my oral exam, I rode the train to Amritsar to visit my grandparents one last time. International travel was expensive, and I didn't know when I might be able to afford to return to India from Europe. In the end, three of my four lovely grandparents would die before I could see them again. I would see only Papa's mother after that.

While in Amritsar, I had strict instructions to outfit myself for Austria. Clothes and shoes—and pretty much everything else—were cheaper in that small northern city. I boarded the train carrying five hundred rupees.

At every stop, amid the offloading and unloading, sellers rush the train bearing omelette sandwiches, onion samosas, milk cakes. Con artists are known to hop aboard, too.

At one of these stops a young man appeared before me: "Pick a card," he instructed. Young and stupid, I did as I was told, handing over the twenty-five-rupee bet demanded of me. When I correctly picked my card from his deck, I'd instantly doubled my wager. "Beginner's luck," he told me, handing me fifty rupees. My heart jumped in my chest. I was hooked. I lost my second try. Then he let me win again, to lure me back. Next time, I bet a hundred rupees. But within a couple of minutes I was down three hundred. Clearly, I'd been had.

I felt so angry, so ashamed, sitting there in my khaki pants and blue plaid shirt, the stupid kid who'd lost his father's money. All around it felt as if passengers were staring at me, wondering how I could have fallen for the trick. I felt like such a loser—the type of guy my father was trying so hard not to raise. I was like a live wire, ready to snap.

I stood up. "Give me my three hundred rupees back," I demanded of the trickster carrying the cards, trying to save face. But he was a grown man.

"Touch me again, we'll pound the shit out of you," he growled. His friends, all in on the con, suddenly crowded in tight, as if to emphasize the point.

I sat back down, shaking. I couldn't tell Papa what had happened. And I knew that the minute I walked through the door back home in Bombay, he would demand an accounting of the five hundred rupees. He did the same thing to Mama whenever she popped out for odds and ends. She'd have to jot down the sixty she'd spent on soap, the seventy she'd spent on new pencil sets for Gauri and me. "You spent a hundred and thirty rupees," he'd say, running the figures in his head. "You should have forty-five left." She'd have to pull out the change to prove it.

In the end, I did what I'm sure Mama did: I fudged the accounts. My new sweater cost three hundred rupees, I told Papa, when really it ran me a hundred. I did the same for my new T-shirts, slacks, and socks. Mama watched me with a raised eyebrow and a sly, knowing smile. I was a bit of a peacock, handsome, with refined tastes, and these were the ugliest clothes I'd ever brought home in my life.

★

Since I was still in Amritsar when my second-year results were announced, Papa and Gauri, my sister, went to Elphinstone to check them for me.

At the start of the school year, each of us would be assigned a roll number. At the end of term, a notice board would go up outside the school—essentially a list of everyone who'd passed. If you'd failed, your name would not appear, a brutal but efficient system.

The college year had been rough, and I was sick with anxiety, terrified my number would be absent from the roll. When Papa called, I could tell immediately from the timbre of his voice that the news was not good. "I'm so sorry, beta," he began gently. "Your number was not on the board."

I was devastated. Papa, surprisingly, was not. By then, he'd grown used to disappointing report cards from me. But he'd watched me in the markets, haggling for a lower price. He'd seen me in his store, upselling his clients, pushing them to the more expensive saris and Salwar suits. He'd come to realize, with con-siderable pride, that I had all the markings of a fine businessman.

And anyway, he reminded me, I was off to Austria in a few months. So what if I hadn't passed?

I didn't see it that way. I was inconsolable. I sat like a slug on the train for the entire three-day return journey. I didn't eat; I didn't sleep. I was a mess. An entire year wasted, I kept thinking. I felt physically ill.

When I got to Bombay, I went to school to pick up my report card. There, I bumped into my friend Naseem. Right away he sensed that something was the matter.

"What's wrong?" he asked.

"I failed," I replied, immediately owning up to it. "I'm so ashamed."

Naseem seemed confused. His roll number came shortly after mine. He'd clearly seen my number on the board. We were pals— he'd checked.

"What are you talking about?" he said. "You passed."

"Naseem, don't joke about this," I said. I was hurting. I couldn't take his needling. Not now. But Naseem was so insistent that he put a hundred rupees on it.

I've never been so happy to lose a bet in my life. It turned out that Papa and Gauri had seen only the first column. Somehow, they'd missed the five columns immediately to its right, where my number was listed. I was livid and elated, all at once.

Papa laughed and hugged me when I told them: "I'm so proud of you," he said. I was bawling. I could leave for Austria with my chin up.

If I'd stayed at Elphinstone another year I could have completed my B.Sc. I wish I had. I take no pride in calling myself a dropout. No matter how well I've done, I'll always consider it a personal failing of mine. Legally, I cannot call myself a college graduate.

But now that I knew what I wanted to do with my life, I was in a hurry to get there. There didn't seem to be a point in staying behind just to collect a piece of paper, especially not with the country on edge.

And so there was nothing left to do but say goodbye. Three days before I left, Shilka called and asked me to lunch in her home. Afterward, she took me to her room. We danced slowly, to Lionel Richie's "Hello," her cheek against my shoulder, her hand in mine. It was her way of saying goodbye. She knew we'd never see each other again.

"If you don't want me to leave, I'll stay," I told her. Truly, I would have. I was crazy for her. But she was unmoved: "Don't," she replied. "You have to go." My heart was broken, but the slow dance, my first, was a sweet parting gift.

I wish I'd left Papa on such good terms. Just days before my departure we'd had one of our worst fights, sparked once again by my long hair. He was insisting on a crewcut. "If you don't cut it, you're not going to Austria!" he screamed at one point, his face mottled with rage. "If he's in my house, he's going to have to abide by my rules!" he hollered at Mama, who was trying to gently intervene.

So I did as I was told. Two days before I left I cut my hair so short I was embarrassed to see my friends, and refused to come downstairs when they popped by to wish me luck.

I wasn't just embarking on a new chapter; I was finding my freedom. For years, my parents, my religion, my society had worked to conform me. "What will people say?" had been the most constant refrain of my youth. Who cares what people think?, I always thought. So what if I don't get into the right school? I knew, even then, that it was all bullshit.

And I knew that in leaving I was free to chart my own course, to express myself, to be who I really am. None of that would have been possible in India. This felt like my flight to freedom.

Waiting, with the wait staff, for the dinner service to begin at the Michelin-starred Post-Stuben restaurant.

Adventures in Austria

I BOARDED THE AIR INDIA FLIGHT on September 24, 1984, as the sun slowly set over Bombay, the steamy night air clinging to me, the city refusing to release its grip. Forward, forward, I pushed away from it.

In those days, you had to cross the tarmac on foot to get to your plane. As soon as I saw my gate I plunged ahead, like a swimmer diving into the deep. "You never even looked back," Gauri would complain, years later. "You were such a free bird—so arrogant, so self-centred, you didn't even bother to check on us, to make sure we were okay."

The truth is, I couldn't bear to turn around. My heart was broken. I was leaving everything I knew. I couldn't take the sight of Mama's tears, of my father's face, frozen in pain. Had I turned around I might never have boarded.

I was nineteen. I had never set foot in an airplane before. I didn't even know how a seatbelt worked—India's rickshaws and trains certainly didn't have them. I was claustrophobic in the tiny, tidy space, so nervous I sweated through my shirt.

It was momentous and terrifying, all at once. All I felt was regret, and a deep sense of foreboding. I closed my eyes and pretended to sleep. I was trying to quell the rising panic, or at least hide it from my seatmates.

In Frankfurt I had to catch a connector to Salzburg. I had practised this again and again with Papa. The old man had actually weighted a suitcase with books and blankets and made me practise carrying it. Papa knew that the trip to Bad Hofgastein, in west-central Austria, would be long, and he wanted me to prepare, to build up some muscle memory. He'd drilled me, peppering me with questions: "How will you find your connector to Salzburg?" And, "How do you find a taxi to Niksu's?" To train me to listen for it, he would recite the call: "Those flying Lufthansa Flight 2-8-9 to Salzburg are now requested for boarding." Thinking back, I can still hear that announcement ringing in my ears.

When I landed in Frankfurt that day, I blessed his foresight. How well he knew his absent-minded firstborn. I ached for him in that moment. I was out of my mind from exhaustion. But I found a board announcing flight statuses, as he'd trained me to, zeroed in on my Lufthansa flight bound for Salzburg, and headed for my gate.

A tiny regional airline serviced the route, and I remember crossing the tarmac thinking, How will we all fit into this tiny plane? It was narrow, with no more than nine seats in total. I sat in the back, smoking, trying to calm my frayed nerves and stop the paranoid track from playing in a loop in my mind: We're going to crash. We're going to crash. We're going to crash. We're going to crash. I am so claustrophobic.

It sounds so simple today. But imagine me then, still a child, really, one who spoke Hindi, and broken English, surrounded by

German speakers, German signs. After thirteen hours, I was barely halfway through my journey to Bad Hofgastein. The final leg took me by bus from Salzburg.

This bus was nothing like India's fume-belching, mechanical monsters who careened around corners at breakneck speeds, luggage tied to the roof, chickens roaming the aisles. They didn't even have doors. Austria was so far ahead of India back then. The brand-new, air-conditioned Omnibusse served as a perfect introduction to my new reality.

By the time I boarded the bus I had been awake for thirty-two hours. But I couldn't peel my eyes from the road. The view from my window was like something from a fairy tale: The snow-capped Hohe Tauern mountains cut through a Windex-blue sky. A few bored sheep, white as clouds, raised their heads to watch us pass. I couldn't believe how few people I saw, how empty the tidy countryside felt. Where is everyone?, I kept thinking to myself. The downshifting of gears as we climbed the manicured mountain road was the only sound to cut the silence. The quiet was deafening, so unlike the constant din of Bombay. And the air. My God, I'd never tasted anything so pure, so sweet! I was used to swallowing diesel and dust all day, then hacking it up overnight.

Bad Hofgastein, in Salzburgerland, in Austria's southeastern Alps, is at the heart of the famed Ski Amadé region, a group of four ski areas known for exceptionally long runs. But the Gastein Valley, which was settled by Bavarian peasants in the ninth century, is most famous for its thermal healing spas, much loved by Mozart's mother, by the Romans, even by Kaiser Wilhelm II, the former German emperor. The pristine thermal waters are still piped into all the valley's major hotels.

Niksu had promised to set up a room for me. He hadn't. He was too busy, he told me. He was immersed in his own new life in Austria, and did not have time to help settle his cousin. I sometimes wonder if this was my payback—a means to teach his pampered, naughty cousin a lesson. Niksu told me I could spend the night with him, but I'd have to find something myself the following day. The next morning I began pounding the pavement, on the hunt for "Zu Vermieten" signs advertising rooms for rent, and cold-calling potential landlords. All I could do was ask for a room, the line I'd prepared in advance.

"Nein, zu viel—No, too much," I'd say, if quoted two thousand schillings. I walked for hours. Finally, a woman offered to take me in at fifteen hundred schillings a month. I jumped at the offer. It wasn't furnished. The worn linoleum and fluorescent lighting did little to brighten my mood. There was no bed yet, so I dumped my bag, arranged my clothes in a pile, and fell asleep, my boundless energy finally—and fully—drained.

That night, the university prepared a special dinner for new entrants: boiled beef tongue. For an Indian boy who'd never even eaten cow—a sacred animal back home—this was going to be a struggle. Then out came a plate of tiny cornichons and pearl onions, rye bread as tough as cardboard, relish and a series of mustards, one more tart than the next.

I'd been raised on white bread and sweet, spicy chutneys. The avalanche of sours was like a revolt: unwanted, unyielding. The meats and charcuterie—all of it served ice cold—upended how I'd always known my foods. In India, as a rule, everything is tabled piping hot.

I couldn't even stand to look at the tongue, but it would have been unconscionably rude to leave it on the plate. The texture was like damp leather. The boiled blood had turned it a deep brown. I'd never tasted anything worse. Even drowned in mustard. I couldn't keep it down. I ran to the washroom and puked. To this day, the thought of the dish makes me shiver involuntarily.

Before I left India, Mama had packed a jar of chili pickles in my bag. When I came home that night I was so hungry I ate the entire jar, plus a loaf of white bread I'd bought along the way.

I was plagued by diarrhea the next day. I made it to class, but it was all in German. The crash course at the Goethe had done little to prepare me for post-secondary coursework. I couldn't understand a thing. So began my Austrian adventure.

Between trips to the bathroom, I realized that I needed a plan to improve my German. I would never survive otherwise. I'd be exiled to Bombay, tail between my legs, to live out my life as my father's apprentice or as a bellhop at the Taj Palace Hotel.

In reality, I was deficient in two areas: I also needed a girlfriend. In the interest of expediency, I packaged the two problems and set out to find a girl who could help improve my language skills.

The next night I went to a nearby pub. I sipped a lager while scanning the room, my eyes resting on a homely, heavier-set young woman. Suzanne was her name. She came from a tiny Austrian town. I didn't even know how to say "kiss" in German. We spent the next six months in bed with a German-English dictionary, practising our new languages, and a bit more.

After six months my German was strong enough that I could say to her, "I'm sorry, but I'm not into this relationship." I knew what a cad I was, but I was in survival mode. Through her, I'd learned passable German, and I'd completely forgotten Shilka.

It was in the wake of Suzanne that I found my first true love: Chirtra Jaganathan, the daughter of a diplomat. She was petite, beautiful, at ease in German, and well liked by all our teachers and classmates. Her dad was stationed in Ankara, the Turkish capital. Her German, after three years in the country, was near perfect— or so it seemed to me.

Because of her proficiency, I think, I teased her. Gripped by jealousy, I sought to belittle her, to try to lift myself up. I didn't understand that then. But I think seeing her fully integrated with our Austrian classmates, with her perfect German, her good grades, made me hate myself more: Why couldn't I get my shit together?

We were friends at first, and used to study together in her room. By then I'd moved out of the first room I'd rented. We lived in a single house with ten dorm rooms, a shared kitchen, and an Austrian caretaker. Then, one day, I kissed her. And she kissed me back. It dawned on me: Shit, I like her. I'd been acting like a child, picking on her because I liked her. Without realizing it, I had been replicating the way my aunties and uncles had treated me as a boy: In teasing her, I was demonstrating my love. Soon, Chirtra became my addiction.

But we kept our relationship a secret. It was like she, the goody two-shoes, was ashamed of me, the party animal. Every night we would wait for everyone to fall asleep, then she would crawl into my room to engage in the kind of marathon make-out sessions you could never keep up past the age of twenty-two. But we didn't tell our friends.

That's the structure my relationships tend to take. I've never been comfortable showing affection in public, holding my partner's hand, openly sharing my love with the world. It's not a function of my upbringing; I've never subscribed to the Hindu obsession with propriety. I love seeing couples share a kiss. But when it comes to me, I've always preferred to keep it to myself.

I couldn't get enough of Chirtra, nor could I understand it. In first year I was making fun of her. By second year, I was falling in love.

The only problem was our mutual friend, Mitul. We'd formed a tight threesome in our first year, and become fast friends. Only Mitul didn't know about Chirtra and me, and it was becoming increasingly hard to ignore that he had fallen in love with her as well. I felt for my endearing friend. I put myself in his shoes. My heart ached for him.

Mitul was a klutz. I've never seen anything like it. If he reached to pick up a cup, he'd drop the plate he was holding in the other hand. In those days, Indian parents chose your profession for you, and Mitul's parents knew he was too forgetful and undisciplined for the sciences. How they ever thought he could succeed in res-taurant management is beyond me.

His other problem was a complete inability to wake up in the morning. I had no problem with early classes. I'd grown up in a home where bedtime came early and morning began shortly after the sun rose. But Mitul was forever running into lectures after they'd started, his hair sticking up in every direction, wearing yesterday's clothes and trying to catch his breath while choking out an apology in broken German.

The day before our service exam in second year, I warned him: "Iron your shirt before you go to sleep. Tie your bow tie, leaving enough room to slip it over your head in the morning. Lay out a clean pair of black pants."

Sure enough, I had to wake him that morning. He'd managed to iron his shirt—or part of it, that is. The collar was a mess. I scolded him, and told him to iron the collar while I ran out to grab us coffees. When I returned he had a giant red welt across his neck. He'd tried to iron his collar with his shirt still on. He failed the service exam because of it. He was badly burned, and in serious pain. In the end, Mitul broke free and found his calling. He's in Australia now, and has done extremely well in computing. He is a brilliant businessman. This was his forte. Hospitality was not.

At night, Chirtra used to hang out with Mitul for an hour, then yawn and say, "I'm tired. I need to get some sleep." When he'd go, I'd enter.

Then, one night, we heard a knock at Chirtra's door. It was Mitul. We panicked. Neither of us would open the door. He'd seen us both enter, and hadn't seen me leave.

Mitul was heartbroken, yelling and screaming, calling me a liar. For six months he refused to speak to me. Finally, toward the end of our second year, he eased up and we rebuilt our friendship.

★

In the first year, we did chef training, learning French techniques— learning how to cut vegetables the correct size, memorizing proper knife styles, mastering the composition of soups and stocks. In second year, we learned kitchen production, big-volume dinner services, and had to choose to specialize in either front-of-house or the kitchen. I chose the former. After third year, we were considered proficient enough to label ourselves "hotel kaufmanns," who could run an establishment on our own.

After each eight-month school term, we had to find a four-month summer practicum. During term Mitul and I would scour area papers every weekend, but we had trouble finding work and the rejections grew disheartening. Plus, it was a lot of work: we had to handwrite and seal every résumé. We had to expand our searches

further and further afield until, finally, we found live-in place-
ments in a tiny town near the Slovenian border.

Mitul worked in front, clearing tables and polishing flatware
and glassware. I was in the kitchen, making and plating salads,
working my ass off. At the time, we still smoked in the kitchen,
chopping and cooking with one hand. Chefs educated the next generation by hollering—an incessant stream of "What the fuck is
wrong with you?" and "You don't know what the fuck you're doing,
you worthless piece of shit." They'd hurtle poorly cut vegetables
from across the room into the sink. Scream at us a half-inch from
our faces, their angry spittle settling on our collars.

I learned a ton from the executive chef, but I can remember
crying alone in my room. In those days, a young line cook's self-
esteem was ravaged by every new kitchen. I passed time in the even-
ings writing Chirtra four-page love letters, full of longing.

The worst part was that my room backed onto the chef's. And
every night, he fucked the brains out of the chambermaid. He was
married, but like mine, his gig was seasonal, and his wife was back
home. His bedposts would bang against the wall behind my head,
a rhythmic torture far worse than what he ever put me through
during the day. At first, I tried to go for a walk when they were at
it. But there was nowhere to go. Pillows, I came to learn, do little
to block sound. Eventually I gave up.

★

The truth is, my time in Austria was also marked by desperation.
Sometimes I felt lost, embarrassed by my thick accent, my immigration status, my poverty, my brown skin.

Papa had given me enough money to survive, no more. To
make ends meet, I waited tables at black-tie, weekend galas, the

type of work my student visa explicitly barred. It was all under the table, but it freaked me out. Had officials discovered it, I could have been deported.

Human beings are meant to express themselves in the language in which they're most at home, their mother tongue. I'm a social person. I love to talk. Living in Austria with a teenage boy's grasp of German felt like walking around with a muzzle. You can't express the depth of what you're thinking. It's like you can't breathe.

The only way to be liked by Austrians, I learned, was to go out drinking with them. But when my Austrian friends brought me along, it sometimes felt like it was done out of a sense of obligation. I felt like a third wheel.

In my third year, I grew deeply depressed. I'd applied for a special immigration status that would allow me to work, but it was endlessly delayed. I'd been surviving on kidney beans—the cheapest, most filling food I could find at the grocery store. Not being allowed to work when you're in your prime, and want desperately to, is like a form of imprisonment.

Desperate, I started eating at the local chapter of the International Society of Krishna Consciousness (ISKCON), better known as the Hare Krishnas. They'd invited me in, having probably sensed my loneliness, desperation. Their job is to watch passersby; if someone takes an interest, they'll come talk to you. Shorn devotees in orange saffron robes would dance and chant in a makeshift temple, lecturing me about a god I knew better than the back of my own hand. If it wasn't so depressing it would have been funny: "Krishna will take care of you," they would tell me.

I was well aware of the omnipotence of the cerulean-skinned

deity. Ours was a spiritual household. Every morning, my grand-mother would read me a scripture. She thought I was like Krishna, who was mischievous and naughty, who loved stealing butter and dancing with girls. My blue eyes were a match for his skin.

Growing up, Bibiji used to take me to both Hindu temples and Sikh gurdwaras to keep me balanced, to show me that there were more ways than just one to pray, to have faith, and that none was better than any other.

The Hare Krishnas listened to me. They fed me chapatis, spicy daal, rajma chawal. The aroma of cumin, turmeric, fennel, and cloves, the bells, the pulsing mridangam drum transported me home, momentarily lifting my crushing loneliness.

They'd call me when I missed a meeting or a meditation. I felt like such a hypocrite. I broke every rule in their loosey-goosey daily to-do list of chants and meditation. I smoked. I drank. I ate meat. I loved coffee. I'd had tons of "illicit sex."

Then came the point when they asked me to go out on the streets to proselytize. "I'm not ready," I told them. It was bullshit. A few days later my visa came through, and I was legally able to work. I left them behind. Was it selfish? Did I take advantage of their kindness? Yes and yes. This was my lowest point. I got through it with their help. Am I thankful for that? Absolutely.

Before I left their fold, they gifted me the Bhagavad-Gita, the Hindu scriptures. I've kept it with me to this day. Whether it's to remind me of their kindness or of my desperation, I still don't know.

Even then, at my worst, I had a vision. I knew I had to become somebody. That's what got me through the indignities of Austria. From within, I found the strength to survive them. I knew where I was heading. I did not allow myself to get distracted, to wallow.

To this day, I have a goal every single day of my life. I cannot be without one. From the moment I wake up to it, I chip away at it, and work toward it. When I've got that goal in sight, nothing can bring me down.

★

There was another reason I hated third year: It marked the arrival of a Malaysian student named George. He was in first year, but a bit older, and started hanging out with Chirtra. She kept telling me they were just friends. But at a certain point, I stopped believing her. Four months in, I confronted George. It was more than a friendship, he acknowledged. George said Chirtra hadn't told him that she and I were dating.

For three days, I holed up in my dorm room. I slept, smoked, and cried; I did nothing else. It was my first experience with betrayal, the first time I'd been cheated on; I felt so hurt, so furious.

Eventually we forgave each other, to a point. We tried to rekindle our relationship, but a wall, built of mistrust, anger, and frustration, had grown between us. In the end, we never were able to repair the damage, and we drifted apart, as if those three years together had never happened. When we graduated that spring, we went our separate ways. We never spoke again.

★

That summer, my luck, at long last, finally changed. I'd responded to a newspaper ad listing a nighttime position at the family-owned Gasthof Post Hotel in Lech am Arlberg, in the Alps. It's a Relais & Châteaux property, a prestigious luxury chain. The Post's co-owner, Frau Kristl Moosbrugger, flew to Vienna to interview me personally. She was a grand old dame, terrifying and precise. She was looking for a night auditor, she explained. The job seemed to boil down to handing keys to drunken guests, keeping a tab for them in the lounge, and learning the delicate politics of not offending the Post's well-heeled repeat customers. The shift ran daily from eleven p.m. to seven a.m.

Austria was hardly teeming with Indians in the 1980s. The tiny foreign community was mostly Turkish. There were even fewer of us in the exclusive resort communities. Still, Frau Kristl seemed to like me, though she wasn't exactly overrun with applicants.

My sole competitor, a native German, was equally qualified. I remember Frau Kristl's lips pursing in a single, pencil-thin line as she sized me up, trying to decide who was better suited for it, he or I.

Mid-interview, she threw out a challenge: The busy four-month winter ski season meant she couldn't offer me a single night off. "Would you be willing to accept these terms?" she asked. I was stunned. Was this even legal? I wondered. But I was desperate. "Of course," I replied. The German had asked for a single night off every seven days. That's how, at the age of twenty-one, my professional career began.

I rode to Lech am Arlberg on the bus. Above us, the jagged peaks were still covered in snow; the alpine meadows were blanketed with flowers, a tapestry of yellows, purples, and whites. It was a hiker's paradise, with hundreds of kilometres of sign-posted trails running in every direction.

From the bus depot, I took a taxi past Lech's famed onion-domed church, past its pastry shops and its stables, crossing the rushing Lech River before arriving at the Post.

It was more striking than Delhi's Imperial Hotel. The hotel's subtle grandeur left me speechless: the carefully appointed flower boxes beneath the windows, the shine of the bright, wide-planked hardwood floors, the crisp white linens and the open fireplaces in the rooms, each of them furnished with local antiques. Frau Kristl and her husband, Franz Moosbrugger, ran it with perfection and predictability. Small wonder that it's a favourite haunt of European royals. The Danish and Norwegian royal families visit annually. Beatrix, queen of the Netherlands, and her husband, Prince Claus, would come every three months. I always served them.

The town's roots date to the 1300s, when farmers settled the nearby valley, clearing the pine forests to create grazing land. Some of it later became ski runs. The hotel was once the town post office, as the name suggests, but the Moosbruggers have owned it since 1937. They weren't the town's only grandees: Several of its old families, including the Schneiders, the Walchs, and the Strolzs, still own Lech's hotels and restaurants, helping to preserve some of the old farming village's charms and to ward off major chain hotels.

Sixteen weeks of back-to-back nighttime shifts is a brutal, unforgiving schedule. I'd never worked a night shift, and it was hard on my body. I'd drink coffee all night to keep me up. By three a.m., my head would be drooping. The hours between three and six were the hardest. But by seven a.m. I was wide awake, which meant I couldn't get to sleep until ten or eleven.

I'd sleep through the day, then wake up late in the evening; I'd grab a quick meal and then head to work. I barely got outside to explore. Even after several months I'd seen nothing of the famed Alps surrounding me. But it was the only way in, and I wasn't about to complain.

I went from Frau Kristl's night auditor to night manager, and then to daytime server in the famed restaurant. But Frau Kristl knew I had a talent and passion for the kitchen. Eventually she allowed me to enter it, under the watchful eyes of Chef Lackner, who ran the Michelin-starred Post-Stuben restaurant.

Candles and antlers decorated the dining room, which had the feel of a hunting lodge. Dishes included Duroc pork with bacon and beans, Beeswax potatoes with trout caviar and saddle of venison. I worked the line as a prep cook, making salads.

Frau Kristl was in her fifties at the time, singularly powerful, and terrifying. Skinny and elegant, she was a blueblood from a distinguished local family of considerable wealth. She ran that fucking hotel like a ship. We were shit-scared of her. When she'd cross her arms and look down her long aquiline nose at us, we'd scurry about like frightened chickens. "Vikram," she'd hiss, "why doesn't table two have its menus?" Or, "Vikram, why is the salad being allowed to wilt on the counter?"

But without that instruction, I would be nothing today. She was always pushing me to be better. She taught me to think three steps ahead. Even as I greeted one patron I'd be scanning the room behind them, noting that table seven needed water, that table twelve was ready to order, that table five was preparing to leave. Frau Kristl taught me to be "on" at all times, to never, ever let down my guard. But the most important thing she ever did for me was to let me go.

★

How many people can say that a single dish changed the course of their lives? That's what happened to me in Lech. I was almost two years into my time at the Post when I was asked to cook for a special guest.

Ivor Petrak, the longtime general manager of the Banff Springs Hotel, was visiting from Alberta as part of a semi-regular junket through the Alps' finest resorts. That night, for his first evening meal with us, the famed hotelier had asked the kitchen to cook him something a bit spicy. I was called in to prepare a dish.

Cooking for Ivor was a big fucking deal. The debonair Czech, an Olympic-calibre former bobsledder, was an industry rock star. He'd managed The Lodge at Smugglers' Notch in Stowe, Vermont, and served as vice-president of the Balmoral Beach Hotel in Nassau. At the time, he was running eight Canadian Pacific properties as a senior CP vice-president. The Banff Springs was his castle.

He'd transformed the aging money loser, convincing CP's board to recommit to the old standards of excellence by throwing a huge pile of money at a costly renovation. Before he arrived in 1971, one guest had ranked the accommodation on par with his "old college dorm room." The hotel was serving bus tours and trade conferences. Ivor put an end to all that.

He'd trained in Lausanne, at the famed Swiss Hotel School, after studying law in Prague. He'd abandoned his studies in his third year after the Czech Coup of 1948, when the Communists took over, and fled. Ivor worked his way up from busboy at the Souvretta House in St. Moritz, to chef trancheur at the Palace Hotel in Scheveningen, Holland, to front-desk manager of the Hotel Brighton in Paris.

I knew none of this as I rushed upstairs to grab the bag of spices I'd tucked into my luggage back in India. All I knew was that Ivor was among the world's greatest hoteliers. And that I was nervous as hell.

I was trained in French cuisine. I had no formal training in cooking Indian food. And though I would occasionally sprinkle garam masala on my sandwiches, I'd eaten it rarely since leaving Bombay.

I chose a goulash, a nod to Ivor's Czech roots. But I never do things by the book, not now in my restaurants, and not back then when I was a chef-in-training. The inventive beef stew was a fusion of Hungarian and Indian flavours—sweet, spicy, hearty. Years later that playfulness would win our restaurants global acclaim. On that day, it brought me to Canada.

Ivor adored it. But instead of sending his compliments to the chef, he offered me a job on the spot. I thought he was joking.

An immigrant himself, Ivor knew that Europe was no place for enterprising global citizens: Its borders were shut tight. "Come to Canada," he told me, plainly. "We need guys like you." A few months later I received a plane ticket in the mail. Ivor had arranged a visa and offered me a six-month contract to work at the Banff Springs.

To this day, I still don't know whether Frau Kristl played a role in the job offer. But a few weeks before Ivor's fateful visit, we'd had a late-night heart to heart.

"I'm a foreigner here," I'd said. "I always will be. I can't ever get an Austrian passport. I can never buy anything, never own anything."

Citizenship, at the time, was based on the principle of jus sanguinis ("right of blood"), and could only be conferred on someone with an Austrian father. Laws barred non-Austrians from owning property.

Frau Kristl saw my talent. She knew that my ambitions were boundless. She knew I needed to move on, somewhere where I stood a chance, where I could make a name for myself. When the offer came from the Banff Springs, I told Frau Kristl I would be back at the Post in six months—in time for ski season. But she knew better.

"Vij Vikram has been chosen as Star Employee of the Month. Vij is a waiter who comes to us on an Austrian exchange program. He's a professional in his field, and our guests have little difficulty recognizing that fact, because of the exceptional service they receive. Vij's professional and helpful attitude have also helped gain him the respect of his co-workers." July 1989.

THE DISH THAT CHANGED MY LIFE

I LANDED IN CALGARY, via Vienna, Frankfurt, and Toronto, on September 24, 1989. The first thing I saw upon leaving the airport was a muskox. What the fuck am I doing here?, I thought to myself.

We were barrelling down a giant, two-lane highway flat as a schilling coin, racing past giant oil tankers, billboards, and suburbs that looked like they might have sprouted the day before. Outside the airport, I'd hopped on a Brewster, a shuttle bus bound for Banff, a hundred kilometres to the west. The dirty jeans and pickup trucks were jarring contrasts to the tidy Alpine idyll I'd left behind.

I arrived in the Rocky Mountain ski town after dark, starving and desperately in need of a beer. It was too late to get into staff housing at the Banff Springs, so I splurged on a thirty-dollar hotel room, further dampening my mood. Then I headed to a dingy, two-dollar pizza joint on Banff Avenue, the first restaurant I saw on the strip. I ordered a root beer off the menu—what I figured must be a popular local style, like a Märzen or a lager. The fizzy pop was so sweet I almost spat it out. But I was too exhausted to find a real beer, so I dragged myself back to the hotel without saying a word to anyone, hoping my mood would be better in the morning.

What brought me around wasn't so much the new day as the Banff Springs Hotel slowly coming into view as I walked up Spray Avenue toward it. The sight of it stopped me dead in my tracks. Perched above a curve in the rushing Bow River, it rose dramatically from a deep-green pine forest like a castle from a medieval fairy tale. I stood there on the road and gazed up at it for several minutes: One day I will conquer you, I promised myself. It was a pledge I would keep.

I often play games with myself to strengthen my resolve. Standing there, I was psyching myself up for yet another struggle. Here I was, a brown-skinned immigrant setting out to find my footing in yet another foreign land. This time I was even further from India. I had already run the new-immigrant marathon in Austria, and I'd found myself at the starting line all over again. I was terrified, and yet somehow full of hope.

With its turrets and towers, the hotel was built in the craggy, Scottish Baronial style. In comparison to the tiny hotels I'd staffed in Europe, it was practically a city, with over 750 rooms and 10 restaurants and lounges. But what drew tourists to the park was the same feature that had first brought them to Bad Hofgastein: mineral baths.

In 1883, two Canadian Pacific Railway employees had come across hot springs at the foot of Sulphur Mountain. This was no discovery: Local First Nations had long been soaking in the spring's sacred waters, which they revered for its healing qualities. Two years later, the Canadian government carved out a twenty-six-kilometre Hot Springs Reserve around them, preserving the land from "sale or settlement or squatting" and establishing the first park in the country.

Ottawa then worked with CPR to develop the baths as a

tourist destination; it was a scheme meant to drive up rail traffic on the expensive new coast-to-coast rail line. Passengers were needed to pay the bills. "If we can't export the scenery, we'll import the tourists," CPR president William Cornelius Van Horne quipped after selecting the site for the Banff Springs Hotel.

It opened June 1, 1888, two weeks after the CPR's Hotel Vancouver, the first two of the country's stable of grand railway hotels, later including the Château Frontenac in Quebec City, the Royal York in Toronto, and the Empress in Victoria, erected to lure Europe's well-heeled.

The hotels went up at a time when Rudyard Kipling was celebrating London's "dominion over palm and pine." That's a more generous view than we held of the Raj's pukka sahibs, who'd come and taken from India what never belonged to them.

★

Hotel staff housing at the Banff Springs granted me a bunk bed and access to a communal kitchen. After orientation, I started in my role as a busboy.

What struck me most about Banff, whose national park boasts three ski areas and a handful of small towns within its more than 6500 square kilometres, was its understated vibe. This wasn't Courchevel, with its Michelin-starred restaurants, or Zermatt with its discretion, or Lech with its royals. There were no celebrities, no pretensions. Here, I knew I could make a mark.

My manager was Peter Blattman, the hotel's focused, driven food and beverages manager. Blattman, orphaned by the Second World War, grew up in Germany's Black Forest, where his parents ran a deli and a small winery. He acquired a taste for fine foods running raw deliveries to area kitchens on his bike.

Rebelling against school at eighteen, Peter apprenticed in restaurants in Germany and then in Switzerland after leaving the
country to avoid mandatory military service. An obvious talent,
he chefed in London and Paris, where he acquired a taste for fine
wines. He studied hospitality, first in Switzerland and then at
Cornell University, the New York State Ivy League school with the
country's top hotel program.

Peter had been at the Banff Springs since 1976, and had
launched the hotel's famed annual wine festival. I caught his attention early with a request to become a dish pig—a dishwasher. I did
it to express my humility and my desire to work hard, to learn the
business from the ground up. The offer was in no way genuine. I
knew full well that Peter would quickly pull me out of the pit,
which he did. But I'd made a mark on him.

To climb the ranks I knew I'd need allies. In studying the
organization's flow chart, I spotted a number of German names
and targeted them first, relying on the language skills I'd developed
in Austria and impressing them with my work ethic. I was charming and tireless, and worked doggedly to develop professional
bonds that would ensure my rise.

Three months after arriving, I was recognized as a Banff
Springs "star employee," an award the hotel gives once a month.
Management took note. Suddenly, I stood out among the hotel's
twelve hundred employees.

I cycled from the kitchen to the floor, a remarkably fast rise
to front waiter.

It was hard work, no question. But to get ahead, you have to
carve out a path for yourself in your mind, then pull yourself up.
I wasn't averse to a few tricks. Once, I literally bumped into the

hotel's general manager on purpose, just to get his attention and to make sure he knew my name.

But I always knew I wanted to work my way back into the kitchen. The only problem was the executive chef. He fucking hated me. He was a mean old grump, a bear of a man known around the hotel as "The Chef," a man who'd haunted the kitchen for decades. He made my life hell.

I'd speak up in meetings. I've always believed that you don't have to say much in a meeting to get noticed. You just have to be smart. At every meeting, I'd bring one or two new ideas: I'd suggest moving dishes to lower shelves to improve kitchen efficiencies, for example, or I'd come armed with a new cleanup procedure. "You don't know what you're talking about," The Chef would scoff. Whenever I spoke up, he would immediately jump in to point out the plan's flaw.

In the end, it didn't matter. The ideas were solid. And Peter supported me. Had he not, The Chef would have trounced me. The executive chef is the number two most powerful figure in the food service hierarchy at the Banff Springs, just below the food and beverage manager. Peter loved me, and he was backing me. And Ivor was pushing me from behind the scenes. "Take care of this guy," he'd told Peter early on. Thanks to Ivor, I was seen as the Banff Springs' new rising star. Ivor showed his hope and faith in me by toughening me further.

Whenever Ivor hosted a major function, he'd say "I want Vikram Vij to serve us." Then he'd scream at me for putting the wine in the wrong place. Once, he kept me on shift until two a.m. He told me he wanted me back in the dining room by five a.m. to prepare to serve breakfast before his group travelled to the airport in Calgary. Rather than go back to my room, I balled up the Rob Roy tartan vest hotel staff wore, curled up under a banquet table, and fell asleep.

Every upward step granted me further recognition from management. I made it clear I wanted to join their ranks, and teased Peter that I would take his job. There was no threat of that, of course. But my ambition was no joke. I was deeply focused on moving up.

But the air up there was thinner, I came to realize. The higher I climbed, the more alone I felt. The more people would criticize my schedules, my choices. The kitchen staff no longer saw me as one of them. My waitstaff was a bit scared of me. I came to understand that management is also a lonely place.

Ivor, a marketing genius, was also a mentor to me. He'd recently sent his sales manager to Japan, where he'd appeared on a popular talk show promoting the hotel, which quickly became a huge draw for the Japanese.

Ivor was then living on Lake Louise, in a cabin that a movie company had built for *Doctor Zhivago*. One of Ivor's favourite guests, a real-life Russian, had visited the hotel a few years earlier. Mikhail Gorbachev had come with a group of Soviet bureaucrats to study Canadian grain production methods. Ivor, at one of his celebrated dinners, got on famously with the amiable Russian, who mapped out for Ivor his grand vision for a new future for the Soviet Union. But the Russians' trip was cut short: News had broken in Moscow that Yuri Andropov, the Soviet leader, had been rushed to hospital. Gorbachev, Ivor's friend, would later go on to trailblaze the Soviet Union's retreat from the Cold War, launching the country on a dramatic new course.

★

Within three years I was promoted to a managerial position with the Banff Springs Golf Course, a massive jump from headwaiter.

I still have my business card—my first—to remind me of the deep sense of pride I felt when I first held it in my hands:

```
VIKRAM VIJ

GOLF COURSE CLUB HOUSE ASSISTANT MANAGER
```

The promotion felt like a victory. But all I could think of was replacing the guy I was reporting to. He was, through no fault of his own, blocking my next upward step. The question was, how?

My manager at the golf course had a relaxed, European style, and he was a drinker. He was mouthy when staff fucked up, and he had a tendency to duck out early. That habit turned out to be my good luck.

Ivor adored the clubhouse, with its panoramic Rundle Mountain views and massive, open stone fireplace. Elk strolled past the windows, delighting tourists. Ivor loved to wine and dine clients late at night when the elegant club was quiet and empty.

One day, I overheard him tell my manager that he was planning to fly in the following Wednesday with the head of Nissan and the Japanese National Tourism board for an intimate evening meal. When that Wednesday, an otherwise quiet night, rolled around, and the last customers were being served around eight p.m., the manager, apparently forgetting Ivor's plans, decided to head home, leaving me in charge.

A half-hour later, Ivor called: They would be nine for dinner, he announced. They would be there by nine. "Mr. Petrak," I interrupted. "I'm afraid the general manager has gone home for the night." Kitchen staff tend to clear out shortly after the manager, and few remained. There was silence on the other end of the line. I could feel Ivor's temper rising. "Don't worry," I interjected. "I'll cook. A table for nine will be ready in twenty minutes." Ivor hung up on me.

The golf course served simple clubhouse fare: burgers and fries. But I made an elaborate salad and served the men individually, explaining the origin of the wine, which was improving Ivor's mood by the glass. My manager was gone the next day. Ivor had called Peter first thing the following morning and ordered him to put me at the helm. He never said why.

That's how, at twenty-six, I became general manager of the $5 million Banff Springs Golf Course. I was twenty years younger than my predecessor and six years out of India. But I didn't grant myself time to celebrate. I focused on building my team.

As a manager, I could eat at any of the hotel restaurants at a 50 percent discount. But I used to haunt the staff cafeteria, watching the servers, getting to know staff, scouring their ranks for talent.

By the time the next season opened, I had built a diligent, driven team around me. We worked like dogs, but we were happy. The comments cards came back with notes about how well "Vikram" had taken care of them, how "incredible" their service had been, all of it noted by upper management.

But every six months I'd have to drive to the nearest immigration office in Calgary to extend my work visa. Thanks to Ivor, this was no problem. He was a powerful local figure whose reach and connections extended to the immigration office. When his key staff needed to re-up their visas, he'd call ahead and make the case that they were essential, securing another six months on our behalf.

But in 1991, out of the blue, Ivor, then in his late sixties, got sick, and died.

Ivor and I rarely spoke of personal matters, and I don't know what he truly thought of his young Indian apprentice. But even when he yelled at me I sensed his endearment and his pride in me. Living up to his sky-high expectations was my thanks to him. To me, he wasn't just a mentor, but a saviour. To this day I think frequently of Ivor, and I often tell my family of the immense role he played in shaping me and my destiny.

When he died, not only did I feel a deep sense of loss, I was also filled with dread. The one man with power, who was able to protect my immigration and work status, had just died.

Indeed, when I went to the immigration office on my own a few months later, officials told me that regulations had changed: I'd been in the country for three years, and would have to return to my "country of origin" to reapply. Just like that, the immigration officer had put my future in jeopardy.

Visa applications were stacked as high as the roof in India's tiny, understaffed, poorly resourced government offices. Officials were getting through less than a tenth of the applications in any given year. The rest got backlogged for years, sometimes decades. A huge portion simply went missing, vanishing into thin air. If I returned to India, I would never get out.

I was at the top of my game. I had a girlfriend. I'd just bought a brand new Volkswagen Jetta. I saw a future for myself here. I broke down and begged the immigration officer to help me. "Canada is my home," I said. He told me he liked me but that his hands were tied. Then his voice dropped to a whisper and he asked me, "Do you have a girlfriend?" I did. "Marry her," he whispered before pushing me out the door.

I returned to Banff broken-hearted.

I was then dating a woman named Maria (not her real name). We'd met working at the hotel. She was petite, gorgeous, with blond hair, blue eyes, big breasts, lots of makeup—the kind of girlfriend I'd always wanted. Everyone adored Maria, her big smile, her open personality. She'd driven west from her home in Cobourg, in southern Ontario, to work the summer season at the Banff Springs as a server. Our relationship was never meant to be anything serious. There had been many Marias in Banff. I was seeing someone else when we started dating.

I was boisterous and loud. Maria was shy, quiet, and seemed awed by me. She seemed more in love with the idea of me—the manager, the exotic past. When summer turned to fall, Maria headed home to Cobourg. My visa had been refused and my panic was growing by the hour. Maria and I kept talking over the phone. "What am I going to do?" I asked late one night, too stressed to sleep. In three and a half weeks I would be forced to leave Canada. "Well," she said, "I could marry you. But you'd have to meet my parents first."

I couldn't afford to fly to Toronto. Maria told me to drive. It was the dead of winter, and I was terrified of the icy prairie highways. But I was out of options and out of time. So on December 21, 1991, I pointed my chocolate-brown Jetta east and set out to meet Maria's parents. I remember stopping to watch the sun set over a frozen field in southeast Alberta—an explosion of pinks and oranges reflecting off the thick white blanket of snow. A row of oil pumpjacks ticked up and down, up and down, like silent metronomes. It was mesmerizing—like a scene from Dallas, plus the ice.

Here I was in this beautiful, wealthy country, hungry, talented. All I wanted was to stay. But I didn't belong, I was being told. Can I really follow through with Maria's offer? I wondered.

But what, really, were my options? I could disappear, out of the reach of immigration officials. I'd earn enough to survive working under the table. If I didn't break a law—or a bone—I'd be fine. Nobody would find me. But I could never earn a paycheque. I could never get a loan. I'd be forced to spend the rest of my life in the shadows, hiding from the government's long arm.

Or I could return to Bombay. But I'd be nothing there, my father's permanent apprentice, selling textiles at a markup. What fate was worse, I wondered: to be a nobody in Canada or in India? At least in India I'd be a legal entity, a human being, not on the run.

I couldn't find the answer among the derricks, so I kept driving. I'd never been to Swift Current, Moose Jaw, Kenora. It was minus thirty-two. I would stop in a hotel and sleep for four hours, leaving the car running because I didn't know how to plug it in. Again and again I'd feel the wind grab my tiny car and try to sweep me off the highway.

Terror aside, I fell in love with Canada while driving from Thunder Bay to Toronto along Lake Superior. Please, God, I thought, let me stay in this beautiful land. When desperation strikes, even Hindu-raised atheists can't help pleading their cases to the almighty.

Finally, after four days' driving, I made it to Cobourg. I'd stopped and shaved in an unheated gas station bathroom as I pulled into town, nicking myself repeatedly in my hurry to get back to the warmth of my car. Maria's parents were waiting for me.

They were lovely people; they'd made us dinner to get to know me. The next morning, Maria walked me around town. A neighbour saw us and complained to Maria's mom that Maria must be so desperate she couldn't even find a white guy. It didn't bother me. By then I'd heard so much worse.

Shortly after Christmas, I had to return to Alberta. I had a check-in with my immigration officer in Calgary I could not miss. Maria and I had made a plan: There was nothing for her in Banff. She had no interest in serving coffee for $4.50 an hour through the ski season. We'd start a new life in Vancouver, where she could study massage therapy and I could finally open a restaurant. She planned to fly out on January 9, 1992. We would marry in a tiny ceremony five days later. It was so fast, so crazy, so stupid. But there was no other way.

My original fourteen-seat bistro on Vancouver's west side, shortly after it opened, in the fall of 1994.

THE BIRTH OF VIJ'S

WHEN I ARRIVED IN VANCOUVER in January 1992, I was greeted by green grass. That alone sold me on the city. I was tired of snow, of ice, of frigid mountain towns. Maria and I married on January 14, two days before I submitted my application to immigrate to Canada. I spent the following day pulling paperwork together for the federal government. Some honeymoon.

Our one-bedroom Vancouver apartment ran us $800 a month in rent, and my savings were quickly disappearing. Maria had a job at Aero Garment Ltd. making corporate apparel, earning barely enough to support us. I was dead bored: Legally, I wasn't allowed to work. But one of my former managers from the Banff Springs was working at Saltimbocca, in Kitsilano, and he got me a meeting with Ken Bogas, the owner.

Bogas offered to allow me to apprentice there; I wasn't paid. I opened and closed the place seven days a week, learning about the local food scene in one of the city's top restaurants.

One morning, shortly after arriving in the city, Maria and I were lining up outside Vancouver's downtown immigration offices at seven a.m., waiting for it to open. She leaned over and whispered loudly, "If you're in Canada, the least you can do is speak English," a reference to the two Filipino women lined up behind us, happily chatting away. I know it wasn't Maria's intention to be cruel. After all, her new husband was an immigrant. She was young, not yet the worldly person she has become. But her words stung. I knew all too well what it felt like to come to a new country, to not be able to speak the language, how daunting and difficult that is to overcome. Learning German in bed with a woman is a far easier task than taking night courses in English at a packed community centre.

I kept my mouth shut, but this was my first realization that Maria and I came from very different worlds. A guy who had struggled as much as I had just to bus tables in Vancouver was not going to mesh with a sweet young woman whose world revolved around her family nest in Cobourg.

We were close friends, but eventually, whatever sexual chemistry had existed between us faded. And we were broke. It was also clear that I was not the kind of husband Maria needed, and I wanted her to be happy. Her marrying me was the ultimate act of friendship, of love that would eventually end in divorce.

There I was, working nine, ten hours a day, with very little money, with no real partner to turn to. I've never felt so alone.

When I got to work that day, Ken joked that I was the "best East Indian waiter I've ever had." I was, of course, the only Indian waiter he'd ever had.

Ken, with his trademark ponytail and salty tongue, was

known for smashing plates and throwing tantrums in Saltimbocca's open kitchen when food was returned.

Bogas lives on Vancouver Island now, working as a landscaper and restaurant consultant. The restaurants Bogas once ran, Saltimbocca, Mangiamo, and Coco Pazzo, are all gone. The restaurant industry is a tough, ugly world.

★

Finally, after twelve months, a letter came from the department of Citizenship and Immigration: I'd been granted landed immigrant status. I was a permanent resident. I could work legally, earn money. I could stay in Canada as long as I wanted.

"Congratulations," the officer told me with a wide smile after our final interview, slamming a stamp onto my visa and making my new immigration status official.

I can't describe how liberating that moment felt. I would never have to prostrate myself again the way I had in the last year. Relief flooded through me. I could feel it in my fingertips. I was free.

That evening, I gave notice at Saltimbocca. I worked another two and a half weeks. I didn't want to leave Bogas in the lurch. When my time there was up, I drove to San Francisco.

I remember getting halfway across the Golden Gate Bridge then pulling over, right in the middle of the busy six-lane highway, and putting my hazard lights on. Behind me horns were blaring, people shouting at me through open windows. I hung over the edge screaming and laughing into the abyss: "I AM FREEEEEE!" Then I ran back to the car, hopped in before the cops could haul me away, and drove off, cackling like a madman. God, it felt good.

A few days later, I flew to India. I remember the wall of humidity that greeted me when I stepped off the plane. I reached down to touch the ground. It was intensely emotional.

I met my sister's husband, Rajdeep Singh, for the first time. He's a cut Sikh—he doesn't wear a turban or a beard. He keeps his hair cut short. I liked him immediately: He's loud, boisterous, and opinionated. He's a bit showy, and he loves to talk. We're a lot alike, he and I. "Kaka," as we lovingly refer to him, now works in Singapore as a shipping executive.

I'd already told my family that Maria and I were over. My father wrote her, telling her how sad he was that things hadn't worked out, how she would always be a daughter-in-law to him. I filed for divorce as soon as I got back to Vancouver.

★

When I returned from India it took me three weeks to find work in Vancouver. I was hired at two pioneering locavore restaurants: Raincity Grill, a Harry Kambolis venture that had just opened at English Bay, and Bishop's, a Vancouver institution in Kitsilano.

Harry Kambolis and John Bishop were true visionaries; each played incalculable roles in the evolution of fine dining in Vancouver. I had the good fortune of learning from them both.

Harry, a New Jersey–born fast-car enthusiast, grew up in a family of restaurateurs: Souvlaki joints, diners, catering facilities, they did it all. When I worked for him, he had just opened Raincity Grill. He'd been studying biology at Capilano University, with vague plans to become a zoologist, when his family convinced him to abandon his studies to run a new space, a greasy spoon they'd bought at the foot of Davie Street, just off the English Bay Beach. Harry launched Raincity Grill in 1993. I joined him a year later, as a manager.

Raincity Grill obsessively showcased fresh, local, high-quality ingredients; it was one of the first to name small farmers, foragers, and fishers on its menus. It was a smart, hugely innovative young restaurant, spotlighting massive Okanagan wine lists long before it was fashionable, along with tasting menus featuring B.C.'s wild mushrooms, heirloom tomatoes, and edible flowers. Harry was so devoted to local foods that he even barred his bartenders from garnishing martinis with lemon twists. He was just getting started.

After I left, Harry went on to launch C and NU, both on the False Creek seawall in Vancouver's Yaletown neighbourhood, both relentless champions of local sustainable seafood. They'd use the entire fish (and trimmings) for stocks and sauces, and innovated with appetizers like "salmon fingers": fried, wild salmon attached to pieces of rib bone. Vancouver Aquarium's Ocean Wise program, which helps consumers make ocean-friendly choices in the grocery aisles, was modelled on C's sustainable sourcing and awareness initiatives.

At Raincity I also met Peter Bodnar, the restaurant's first sommelier. Peter taught me everything I know about wine. He used to give me blind taste tests at eleven a.m., lining up five small glasses of wine, compelling me to smell them, to jot down tasting notes. He'd never put you on the spot—he would guide you, and help you identify flavours. He taught me to empower the customer. These days, when I push my customers at Vij's to note the cardamom and bold chilies in their dishes, I think of Peter. As I became more proficient in my understanding of wine, he allowed me to choose our nightly wine lists, gently critiquing as he helped me select perfect pairings to accompany the evening's menu.

But while Raincity helped pay the bills, Bishop's, long considered to be among Vancouver's top restaurants, was the more prestigious position. John Bishop, a Welsh native, was seen as the granddaddy of the city's farm-to-table movement. When he opened on Fourth Avenue in 1985, fine dining in Vancouver meant basing menus on foods from anywhere but B.C.: mahi mahi from the Tropics, Icelandic scampi, Dover sole, New Zealand lamb. B.C.'s rich bounty was disdained. Restaurateurs were still importing their mushrooms from Germany, their scallops from Asia, their berries from California. There were no local spotted prawns or cracked crabs on menus. It was insane!

Inspired by Alice Waters of Berkeley's Chez Panisse, John relentlessly sourced and showcased local, seasonal foods, offering Dungeness crab–filled ravioli, smoked sablefish, and rack of lamb from B.C.'s northeast Peace River region. But I couldn't earn any money there. John Bishop could only offer me lunch. To start, I was a table runner.

There's no one lower in a restaurant. But I was willing to take that giant step down just to get my foot in that door. The Bishop's name was résumé gold. It's like getting a Phys. Ed. degree from Harvard. The lowly degree doesn't matter: You're a Harvard grad. I was thinking strategically. I knew I wanted to open my own restaurant. I was hungry, impatient. I didn't want to wait. But I first needed to understand the local restaurant industry. Bishop's allowed me to train with the best in the game.

John hired me because I had European experience. He knew I could be trusted, and he could sense how keen, ambitious, and energetic I was. He loved that I immediately established meaningful friendships with his kitchen staff. That was necessary for my job. I understood that a kitchen is like an infantry unit, and relies on camaraderie.

I had to liaise with the kitchen to make sure the customer's table was properly set for the course, and to hustle food from the back to the table. Table eight ordered two coffees and a Death by Chocolate dessert? Table twelve needed their sparkling water topped up? It was my job to attend to their needs.

John was a crucial mentor. The most important lesson he taught me was an absolute devotion to guests. With a nimble memory and the ability to treat every customer like the most important person in the room, John became known in Vancouver almost as much for his hospitality as for his culinary excellence.

He treated the restaurant as an extension of his own home. I used to sit and watch him work the room: People would be eating their salad courses, and he'd lean in with a big, warm smile, offer a little bread, and say a few words of welcome. "Oh my God, we were personally served by John Bishop," customers would whisper across the table. They loved it.

Even now, I still do this at Vij's: If I see somebody really enjoy-ing their meal, I'll grab a chutney and say, "Try the pork belly with a bit of mint mango chutney." I don't talk politics with them. I won't ask about their lives. I'm not there to chit-chat. It's strictly about the food—to impress that I'm there to serve them, and that I'm deeply thankful they've done me the honour of eating at my res-taurant. This I learned from John.

The funny thing is, John, now in his seventies, learned that service ethos from his mentor, Peter Barry, when he was getting his start in the industry. John met Peter, a Swiss-trained hotelier, when the two were working at the same small Welsh restaurant. John was then still training as a chef. Peter was a manager—affable, charming, open. He was everything John was taught not to be.

At the time, John was studying French cuisine. The service end of the French method is relentlessly formal. He was taught that the food alone is important, that under no circumstance do you address your guests, that you deliver their plates and quickly retreat, allowing them to enjoy the food in peace.

Peter was doing the complete opposite: He was hosting in the truest sense of the word, forming deep and meaningful relationships with his customers. And he was being rewarded for it with their loyalty. John realized, watching Peter charm his guests, laugh with them, how badly he'd misunderstood the front-of-house role. So he course-corrected, following Peter's lead. The two would remain close for the rest of Peter's career, and went on to partner together in a restaurant venture in Kinsale, County Cork, Ireland.

John will tell you that he never saw what he did as business, as a strictly money-making scheme. To him, the point of it all, or at least the joy of it, was in forging relationships, in having fun. I try to do the same in my restaurants, and have formed lifelong friendships with many of my loyal customers.

But behind his gentle facade, John, a perfectionist, could have a quick temper. This is something else we share. When he walked beyond those swinging doors at the back of Bishop's, John would quietly fume: "Why doesn't table six have enough butter?" He could become enraged over the slightest mistake—when you dropped off a drinks order, say, and handed the white wine to the wrong person. Before leaving the kitchen, you had to memorize the order. Asking "Who ordered the chicken?" at the table was strictly verboten. He was exacting. I'm no different with my own staff today. This, too, I learned from him.

★

By then it was 1994, and Papa was worrying about me. I was in Vancouver, alone. And professionally, I seemed to have taken a step back. He wanted me to set out on my own. But his mother, my last living grandparent, was dying from cancer. "Papa, don't come," I kept telling him. "Stay with Dadiji. This can wait." But my grandmother was meanwhile urging him to go to me, to help her cherished grandson. Papa was caught between us. She died August 1, 1994.

On September 10, my parents arrived from India with a three-month visa and a mission to "settle" their son. For Mama, this meant providing me with the love and emotional support she worried I was lacking. For Papa, it meant helping me set up a restaurant of my own, and finding me a wife. With just ninety days to do it, he was in a hurry. By December 24, 1994, both goals had been achieved.

The night Papa arrived, we were sitting on the couch, drinking hot chai spiked with cardamom, when he nonchalantly said, "I brought you $23,000."

"What?" I practically shouted. "How did you get that past Immigration?"

"They didn't ask," he said, with a mischievous grin, lifting his palms up beside his ears. "I didn't tell."

It turned out that Papa had carried the cash—in US$100 bills—in a brown paper bag tucked into his luggage among his kurtas and slacks. I had to blink away my tears. "Thank you, Papa," was all I could get out. "Of course," he said. "What did you think? I wasn't going to help my beta?"

With him, business decisions were made from the gut and were done, above all, to elevate the family. He was doing what his grandfather and his uncles had done for him: help him establish a foothold in the industry. The rest was on me.

The first step was to find a suitable space. For weeks, Papa and I hunted for the best location. While I was at work he would dial up realtors and scout locations, then show me what he'd found. But realtors seemed to show us nothing but dead zones on hidden side streets and tiny storefronts. None of it was suitable. Our success hinged on finding the right location.

I liked the high-end South Granville Street area. Papa favoured bustling Broadway Avenue. We compromised, settling on Café Arabia, a falafel shop on Broadway and Granville. Or rather, Papa did.

I didn't want to open a casual takeout joint. On this, I was adamant. I wanted to open a proper restaurant. We argued over it one morning. Then I left for my shift at Bishop's. When I got home that afternoon, Papa told me he'd bought out Café Arabia's lease agreement. I was shocked.

"Location," Papa told me, "is everything." He loved the hustle and bustle of the major intersection where the two arteries meet. In the streams of people strolling past, he saw the potential for a healthy walk-in business. So while I felt hurt that Papa would do something so rash, something I'd explicitly said I didn't want, his reasoning was sound.

And in the end, I understand my father—who he is, how he behaves. Papa is the kind of guy who, once his mind is made, it's made. It's not worth arguing with him. It's "What are you waiting for? Let's go! We're moving to Bombay, everyone! Get ready!"

Any surprise or hurt I might have felt was subsumed by a feeling of immense pride. After all, there I was, Vikram Vij: restaurant owner. All my dreams had finally come true. I knew I could make something great of that dingy little café.

I'd managed to save $10,000 of my own over the past three years, so with the cash Papa smuggled in from India, our combined budget for a restaurant was $33,000. The lease for Café Arabia cost us $32,000. We paid in cash; the former owner counted out every bill. But I needed $5000 more to get the new place off the ground. I was just a permanent resident at the time. I knew that securing a bank loan would be unlikely, so Papa borrowed the rest from a family member in Bombay.

The following day I gave John Bishop notice. In all, I'd worked for him three years. He scoffed at my plans to venture out on my own. It's not that he wanted me to stay, though he did. He just didn't want me to get hurt. He knew how hard, how ugly, how unglamorous the industry was, how tight the margins were, how many first-timers fail out of the gate, how many dreams are crushed, how unlikely my success was. "Don't do it," John implored. I ignored him. My mind was made up. I wasn't there to ask his permission.

★

Later, I would adopt John's team-system service style. But at first it was a one-man show, with me prepping, cooking, serving, and cleaning up. For the first few weeks, we ran the place as a Lebanese joint. I kept the menu intact. I couldn't afford to change it. Café Arabia had a handful of regulars, and I couldn't risk losing their business. I'd spent two weeks training under the previous owner, a too-quick lesson in chicken taouk and donair kebabs.

But rice is rice. And pita is basically naan. "We bought a business, not a restaurant," Papa would say. It didn't matter to him whether I was selling falafels or samosas. But within two weeks, I was getting restless.

Soon, I started experimenting. I needed to be authentic, to serve what I knew, the flavours of my youth, the spices of my dreams. I started infusing the menu with Indian seasoning and techniques, "Indianizing" the menu. I'd spike the tabbouleh salad with a little garam masala. It paired nicely with the lemon juice and cracked pepper. I added heat to the hummus. To the chicken, I'd add a little curry for a bit of sweetness. I'd infuse the lamb with mango powder and lemon juice, creating my own unique style.

I wasn't uncomfortable cooking Middle Eastern. And with my dark skin and accent, customers seemed to assume I was Lebanese. Vancouver was a different city at the time. People then thought parsley was exotic. Few understood the intricacies of the Orient's regional cuisines—Afghan, Indian, Lebanese. To many, it was all ethnic. And so were we.

Then I took it a step further. One Friday, we shuttered the place for the weekend and repainted. We picked up a new sign we'd had made. We bought a chalkboard, where we advertised the new menu.

On Monday, when we reopened, Café Arabia was gone. Out front, there was a new sign: "Vij's." But I couldn't afford to go all in; I needed to keep some of Arabia's customers. The hardest part of this business is getting a customer. I felt that if I could get them in the door, they'd appreciate my cooking. So for the time being we continued to sell Indianized Middle Eastern fare.

People assume that because I'd worked at Bishop's, I was just following his lead with the new name. But it wasn't a reference to me. It was done to honour Dadaji. Here was his dream, finally realized. I poured myself a scotch and toasted my grandfather. If only he could have lived to have seen it.

In a way, I'd come full circle: For years, I'd been living in foreign countries, trying to infiltrate foreign cultures. And now here I was, a business owner in a country I called my own. I felt comfortable enough to introduce my culture and cuisine to my new home.

The only problem was the electric stove. And it was a big problem. The previous owner had assured us that all we'd need to do was apply for a change-of-use permit, then we could bring in proper equipment. He was lying. And we didn't do our homework, a major error that I would never repeat. We didn't have the requisite gas hookups or exhaust system to qualify for a full licence, which seriously limited the type of cooking I could do legally.

So Mama stepped in. Until I could get the proper stoves, she would cook the dishes at home, she said, and then she and Papa would ride the bus in from Richmond. For the next eight weeks, that's exactly what we did. Only years later would Mama admit that people made fun of her on the bus—this little Indian lady with pots of hot curry wrapped in plastic bags between her knees.

In the evening, Papa and Mama would help me clean up. I couldn't afford to hire anyone to help. At the time, my parents and I were living together in Richmond, renting an $800-a-month apartment on Cambie Road. When we returned to their flat each night, Papa and I would put back two or three whiskeys and plot the next day.

★

By then, my parents had been in Vancouver for several weeks. I'd come back from a long, exhausting day's work at eight or nine every night, having bused home, looking forward to a few minutes' solitude. Instead, a young, hapless Indian girl would be seated on my couch with her entire, gawking family.

My father, it turned out, had put an ad in the paper, advertising his bachelor son like a second-hand vacuum.

"What the hell, Papa?" I finally said to him. "You need to stop doing this. You're raising their hopes."

Inevitably, the parents would call back and say, "We liked the boy." I was dead set against an arranged marriage.

"We need to find you a girl," Papa said, patiently but forcefully.

It's not that I didn't want to meet anyone. But I wasn't remotely interested in a traditional Indian woman. I was liberal. I drank, I smoked. I was divorced, for Christ's sakes.

But they were firm: My marriage to Maria was over, and now the time had come to find someone new, to settle down and start a family.

They hadn't seen me in years. To them, I was like any other doting Indian son. I just happened to be living in Vancouver. But the truth was, I was nothing like their friends' boys. I had been out of India for more than a decade. I'd made something of my life. I was a firm believer in gay rights. I was a feminist. I had lots of sex. To me, dowries and arranged marriages were antiquated, backward traditions, best forgotten.

They didn't understand any of this. That was the moment I realized, not without sadness, that they no longer knew their own son. I'd love them as I always had, of course. But a gulf had grown between us that I knew could never be bridged. We were like two banks of a river: we're always close, but we'll never meet.

★

At the time, Bishop's executive chef Michael Allemeier's wife was studying sports psychology at the University of British Columbia. They lived in the Vancouver suburb of Coquitlam, and shared a car. Every morning, after Michael dropped his wife at UBC for nine, he'd have nothing to do until his shift at Bishop's started at two-thirty. So Michael would come hang out at my kitchen and cook

The yard outside our family home in Delhi, shortly after we moved in, in 1971. I was seven then. Sonia and her family lived just across the street.

Visiting a hill station, one of the picturesque, mountain towns the Brits founded as refuges from India's oppressive summer heat. I'm here with my father.

On holiday in Nainital, in the eastern Himalayas. That's my cousin—Gauri and I called him "Poppy Uncle."

Sonia Sarovar, my first love, and her younger brother. God, was I crazy for her. That the feeling was so rarely reciprocated made Sonia all the more attractive to me.

Roshan Lal Vij, my grandfather; "Dadaji," as I knew him. "Beta," he used to tell me, "one day, I want you to open the finest restaurant in the world."

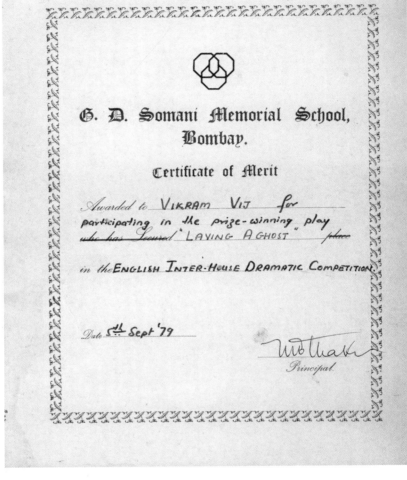

G. D. Somani Memorial School, Bombay.

Certificate of Merit

Awarded to VIKRAM VIJ for participating in the prize-winning play who has Secured "LAYING A GHOST" place

in the ENGLISH INTER-HOUSE DRAMATIC COMPETITION

Date 5th Sept '79

Principal.

I've loved acting my entire life. I earned this award for a play I wrote; I played a ghost in the one-man production.

विद्या सर्वार्थं सिद्धये

Tel. No. 212587

G.D. SOMANI MEMORIAL SCHOOL Cuffe Parade, Bombay-400 005

Your Ref :

Our Ref :

Dated

Dated **20th June, 1980.**

TO WHOM IT MAY SONCERN.

Vikram Vij joined this School in June 1977
and left in April 1980, after completing the
Secondary School Certificate Course.

Vikram has a vivacious personality, who becomes
completely engrossed in any activity assigned
to him. He is conscientious about his studies
as well. He is very interested in dramatics, both
Hindi and English and is a good actor.

He is keenly interested in sports and has
represented the School in cricket and table-tennis..
As a Nature Club member he has attended a number of
national camps.

He bears a good moral character. His date of
birth, according to our School records is
22nd December 1964.

House-Master
ABHAYA

J.A.S.Newton,
PRINCIPAL.

*After leaving Delhi when I was twelve, I enrolled at G.D. Somani school. I worked
hard there. The confidence that success instilled in me was intoxicating.*

To make ends meet while I was studying in Austria, I spent every weekend serving at black-tie gala dinners.

I launched my career at the Gasthof Post. The elegant, graceful hotel, nestled in Austria's central Alps, is a favourite haunt of Europe's royals.

The Banff Springs' serving staff, in the hotel's red tartan. I'm in the middle row, second from the right.

At twenty-six, I became general manager of the $5 million Banff Springs Golf Course. I was 20 years younger than my predecessor, and six years out of India.

*Gauri, my sister, on her honeymoon
with her husband, Rajdeep Singh. He's
loud, boisterous, and loves to talk; we're
a lot alike, he and I.*

*Gauri and Rajdeep's wedding.
They live in Singapore now,
where Rajdeep works as a
shipping executive.*

The first and only time in my life I was skinny. "You duped me with your fatness," Meeru likes to joke.

Together with Shanik, Meeru, and Nanaki at Meeru's first annual Joy of Feeding, an international food festival of home cooks and a fundraiser for the University of British Columbia's sustainable agricultural programs in May 2011.

CURRY ART GALLERY

Our first menu at Vij's 11th Avenue.

Salmon in golden puff bread with sesame-coconut sauce   6½

Grilled zuchini with pomegrante sauce and chick pea salad   6

Jackfruit in spring onion curry with couscous   6

Vegetable semolina halva with mint-mango chutney   6

Homemade paneer in tomato and fenugreek marinade   6½

Indian squash dumplings in tomato cream curry with naan   13

Eggplant, bell peppers and potato curry on parantha   12½

Mild green chilli and cilantro chicken curry with saffron rice   14½

Bengali style cod on basmati rice with raita   14½

Lamb in fennel and tamarind curry on new potatoes   15

Grilled, marinated pork chops in garlic curry with naan   15

Oven roasted quail in onion seed curry with naan   16

Rapini and homemade paneer, red bell peppers with chapati   14

Desserts   4½

Ginger-lemon drink   3¾

Storm Brewery: India Pale Ale   4
                 Scottish Ale   4

Wine: Bottle 29   Glass 5¾

   Pierre Sparr Pinot Blanc
   J. Lohr Baymist Riesling
   Nichol Vineyards Pinot Gris
   Domaine Combret Chardonnay

   Quailsgate Old Vines Foch
   Joseph Drouhin Beaujolais Villages
   Montevina Cabernet Sauvignon

Items on our first menu at Vij's 11th Avenue.

A more recent iteration of our Vij's menu. The playful elephant lanterns are used to light our cozy dining room.

June 24,2016

- **Good Morning Ms and Mr Vijs:**

- **Congrats in your opening after 6 years.**

- **We like your food,we like your decor**

- **We at Pacifica ask you to redirect the smell of your 7 days/week of your stinky prep.6-8AM when traffic is good and the air is clear we get terrible smells into our air distribution throughout all 3 buildings.There is a way to fix it and please comply.**

- **Parking on the street has become a nightmare on both sides and I am suggesting to have Valet parking, which will make your location that much more sought after.**

- Please be a good neighbour and perhaps have an open house by invitation ONLY for all PACIFICA owners/renters that endured 6 years of having to see how this building was used as a retreat for many undesirable people.

- Looking forward to your positive reply,

The delay in moving into our new location on Cambie Street irked at least one of our neighbours.

PRIME MINISTER · PREMIER MINISTRE

Ottawa, Ontario
K1A 0A2

MAY 0 6 2016

Dearest Vikram + Kam

Dear ~~Mr. Vij and Staff~~:

Thank you so very much for hosting the Premiers, Aboriginal leaders and myself at Vij's in early March, and for making it such an unforgettable experience.

It's not only the amazing lamb popsicles and delicious wine that draws me to Vij's, it's the incredible hospitality displayed by the team. I sincerely appreciate the care and skill that goes into crafting the food, atmosphere, and service. As you may know, this was not my first time eating at the restaurant, and it certainly won't be my last.

Thank you once again for accommodating us, and I hope to visit again soon!

Sending you all my very best,

Sincerely,

Mr. Vikram Vij and Staff
330 77 West 8th Avenue
Vancouver, British Columbia
V5Y 1M6

Prime Minister Trudeau first visited our restaurant when working in Vancouver as a young teacher. In the spring of 2016, he hosted a dinner with the country's premiers and several Indigenous leaders—the first First Ministers' meeting in over a decade.

Greeting Prime Minister Justin Trudeau outside Vij's in March 2016.

My frequent visits to India continue to inspire my cooking.

with me. We'd make mulligatawny soup or perfect a recipe he was hoping to trial at Bishop's.

In this way we'd cook the mornings away, cracking jokes around my pathetic four-burner stove. By then, Michael was relatively well known in Vancouver: "That's Michael Allemeier," some would whisper when they spotted him in my kitchen. I consider Michael one of the finest chefs Canada has to offer. He's focused. He loves his job. And he's the best teacher you'll ever find. After chefing at some of Western Canada's finest restaurants, Allemeier became an instructor of culinary arts at SAIT Polytechnic, in Calgary.

During the lull, from two-thirty to five, after the lunchtime rush, I used to sit down and try to dream up ways to increase revenue and generate more business. I wrote to each of the food reviewers in Vancouver in longhand, one by one: "You may not remember me from my time at John Bishop's," I'd write, "but I've just opened up my own restaurant on Broadway . . . "

After four months, business was still slow. I was bringing in $95, $97 a night. Sometimes I would ring in an order of naan bread just so I could tell myself I'd cleared $100 in sales, my break-even. I was cheating myself to try to boost my self-confidence. But I knew I wasn't getting anywhere. They were dark days.

Finally, one wet, dark, miserable November night, sometime after my grand reopening, my phone rang just as I was closing up for the evening. "I'm Robin Mines," said the woman at the other end. "You wrote to me, and I'm hoping to review your new restaurant." Mines, who wrote for the *Westender*, was one of the more influential critics in town.

"How far are you?" I asked, trying to hide the panic from my voice. "About fifteen minutes from you," she answered.

I thought, Tell her to come back during the daytime. But my gut knew better than to take the risk.

"Great," I said, slamming the phone into the receiver. I think I hung up on her.

Then I fucking tore around the restaurant, throwing the lights back on, pretending we were still open. I was thrilled and horrified all at once: I'd been about to close the place and had no food left. Every day we ordered just enough meat and produce to get us through a day. I couldn't afford to let any go to waste.

I gave Robin my hot Indian hummus, my take on tabbouleh with cilantro, a garam masala–spiked donair. On the side, I served pickles cured in lemon juice. Mines left without saying a word about how she felt about the food, but I could tell she liked the experimentation.

Around the same time, in another meaningful telephone call, I was introduced to Meeru Dhalwala. Urmil, her mom, who was better known by her nickname, Omi, had been a close childhood friend of Mama's in Ambala, outside Delhi, but they hadn't spoken since 1965. Omi lived in Washington. When Mama had contacted her she didn't realize that her old friend was in D.C., not B.C.'s Pacific Northwest neighbour state.

Still, they talked, quickly falling back to the banter of their lost youth. In Omi, Mama confided her fears for her divorced, loser son. And Omi, meanwhile, complained about Meeru, her older daughter, a divorcée. It didn't take long for the conniving old pals to hatch a plot to introduce us. The strangest part is that it worked.

Something about Meeru—her confidence, her strength, her sense of self—intrigued me. We hit it off over the phone, so I invited her to visit me in Vancouver during American Thanksgiving in 1994.

I greeted her at the airport with a kiss. It was a blind date, effectively. But I was immediately smitten. Meeru is beautiful, lean and angular. Her freckled face is inquisitive, serious, and ringed by soft black curls. She is supremely confident and self-assured, with a sharp style.

I noticed that she walked with a slight limp, and asked her if she had broken a toe. "No," she answered. "Why?" I kept quiet and smiled to myself. I was glad she was not too perfect to be true.

She was quite unlike any other woman I'd ever met. That's what truly drew me in. Meeru knows exactly who she is, and she's unafraid to tell the world what she thinks.

She's a thinker, a reader. She's always got several books on the go. She never misses *The New Yorker* or *The New York Times*. After getting a bachelor's degree in French literature, she interned with Amnesty International, campaigning against the death penalty, then with the National Academy of Sciences in D.C., working with its Committee on Human Rights. She went on to get an M.Sc. in development studies from the University of Bath, doing fieldwork in India's urban slums.

Before meeting her, I'd crash-dieted and was rail-thin for the first and only time in my life. I was supremely confident—cocky, really—and told her I'd done a bit of modelling—a reference to a long-ago motorcycle ad I'd shot while a student at Elphinstone in Bombay, my one and only modelling gig. I must have been a bit awed by her education, her poise. I was trying to keep up, in my own clumsy way.

To say Meeru was underwhelmed by the sight of Vij's would be to massively understate her reaction. She was thirty. She'd been living in downtown Washington for eight years. She travelled back and forth between D.C. and Manhattan, where her younger sister, Ritu, worked in the art scene. She visited London regularly. She had money. When I told her I'd just opened a bistro in Vancouver, she thought, Okay, we're on the same page.

Then she got there. My strip-mall bistro smelled of stale curry. There were holes in the ugly maroon carpet. My dad was helping serve. My mom was busing in curry by the potful from the suburbs. The place had fourteen seats, and no one was there. What the fuck is this?, she thought when she first saw it. Bistro? It's a fucking hole in the wall.

But Meeru could also see how incredibly proud I was of Vij's, how much I believed I could take this dingy little diner and make it a success. And although she was certainly taken aback by the state and size of my "bistro," she fell in love—with me, with my passion, my ambition, my sense of pride in my work. She could look beyond the dirty, ratty carpet and see what I already saw: a future.

The entire weekend I kept telling her I couldn't wait for Wednesday, the day the *Westender* would hit the newsstands. My skin was tingling in anticipation. I knew that whatever Mines wrote would either make or break me.

In all, Meeru stayed five days. In the afternoon she'd come to the restaurant and hang out with me until I finished at seven, then we'd head to Spanish Banks to get to know each other over a pizza and a bottle or two of wine by the beach. I wanted more, but my parents were home. We'd stay out until six or seven in the morning. We were like teenagers. I couldn't get enough of her.

By day five, when Meeru was scheduled to fly home to D.C., she was falling for me. It scared her. I could tell how she felt. I knew

I wanted to be with her. This is the girl I'm going to marry, I remember thinking.

I was driving her to the airport when I stopped suddenly and turned to her: "If we get serious, there's something you need to know about me. I'm very pro–gay rights, and I'm pro-choice. If you're not, I can't be with you." I needn't have worried. She felt similarly.

I'm divorced, Meeru thought. And I've never dated an Indian. She wasn't even sure she trusted Indians! She'd fly home, she thought; she'd continue her work. We'd try out a long-distance relationship. If we somehow made it work, she'd consider moving to Vancouver.

But I wanted none of this. I didn't want a long-distance relationship. I'd just opened a restaurant. I needed to focus everything in me on my new business. At the airport, I told her I wanted to give her the rest of my life, right now, or end it.

It took Meeru all of about two seconds to make up her mind outside the security gate at YVR. "What the hell," she said. "Sure."

She later told me she'd rather be the eighty-year-old who'd taken a flyer on the Indian boy she met in Vancouver. She doesn't want to look back at life and wonder about the missed opportunities she was too fearful to try. "You move where life takes you," she'll say with a shrug.

The very next day, Robin's review hit the newsstands. Vij's was "making its mark on Broadway," she wrote. A powerful statement. I was overcome with joy seeing my name, my restaurant, gently celebrated by the newspaper.

After twenty-five years in the business, I'm unfazed by reviews. But the first is different. To this day, I can recite Mines's piece by heart, like the poems you learn as a schoolboy. "Euro techniques,

Indian spices, and colourful presentation combine to make dishes that are unlike anything you've ever tasted," she wrote.

Her words filled me with confidence. My youth's forgotten spices were like notes in music. I knew it was in them that I would find success.

Meeru and I married on Christmas Eve, 1994, at a suburban chain hotel. December 24 was my only day off, and Meeru gamely agreed.

"MAKING A MARK ON BROADWAY"

WE CAN NEVER LOOK AHEAD to the future—not our own, not anyone else's. In real life, there is no skipping pages. The essential beauty of this journey, and at the same time perhaps its most frustrating part, is that you can never know what will come next.

But this I do know: Had it not been for Robin's review, I would not have survived. I would have returned to Bishop's, embittered, my tail between my legs, the one-time proprietor of yet another short-lived Vancouver restaurant. At the time, I was on the verge of shuttering Vij's. We could only seat fourteen. We lacked the equipment and licences to run a proper restaurant. Overhead was higher than anticipated, and I was still cooking on a fucking electric stove.

This felt like rock bottom. I had no more cash on hand. Papa had given me everything he had. I'd borrowed all I could. I was tapped out. There were no more doors to knock on. Things were so bleak I'd started encouraging customers to order dishes with higher profit margins.

"Try the lamb," I'd say if someone ordered the chicken—not because it was the superior dish, but because I knew that the profit on the lamb was a dollar more. And if, at the end of the day, we'd made only $10 more, it put us $10 closer to profitability.

Most of this was my fault. It was my first business, and I made a lot of rookie mistakes. I'd leased a restaurant space zoned for retail, which meant we couldn't serve alcohol, driving away a ton of traffic. Who wants to go out on a Friday night and order a Coke with dinner?

The venting system was insufficient, and the landlord was a huge prick about the smells. He used to bang on the wall and yell about the scent of curry seeping into the neighbouring hair salon. I didn't blame him. Who wants to get their hair done where it reeks of chickpeas and masala? But I couldn't do a thing about it. Indian food has an intense odour. The ginger, onions, garlic, and roasted spices that kick off a curry throw a big aroma and it only builds from there.

I hadn't spent enough time pricing menu items. I'd sell $1000 worth of food, then realize I hadn't made any money at all. I'd blown $400 on food costs. The rest went to pay for the linens on the table, the cost of dry-cleaning them, the odd broken dish (or twelve), the steep Broadway rents. But I was a quick study. I learned to inch the prices up from $6 to $6.25 for chicken curry, or from $7 to $7.50 for lamb. These markups were meant to help cover some of the hidden costs I hadn't yet learned to factor in.

But Robin changed all that. The day her review came out, six people showed up in the evening, when normally from four to six p.m. not one customer would come through the doors. I had to scramble: Shit, I didn't have enough falafels for everyone. I was cursing and sweating, trying to stretch what little food was left while trying to feign being at ease. I was fucking panicked. And after Robin broke the ice among reviewers, more and more started stopping by, praising the upmarket Indian cuisine, the excellent service. The more good reviews we got, the more new customers found their way to us.

It was around then that I met Ashwin Sood, one of my first regulars, who would become my closest friend. Birmingham-born and Calgary-raised, Ashwin is a charismatic musician and drummer. He's played with Sheryl Crow, Rufus Wainwright, Stevie Nicks, Jason Mraz. The list goes on. At the time, he was engaged to Sarah McLachlan, the famed Vancouver singer-songwriter. He'd met her when he was playing with Lava Hay. It was years before I realized what a big deal Sarah was.

I have to admit, I'm utterly clueless when it comes to celebrities. I work so hard, I don't have time to see new movies, read the paper's entertainment section, watch TV. I leave it to Meeru to let me know when a celebrity wanders in. "What are the Red Hot Chili Peppers?" I once had to ask her.

But back to my chance first meeting with my best friend. It was lunchtime, and Ashwin had been walking along Broadway looking for a place to grab a bite. The aromas wafting from the restaurant stopped him in his tracks: That smells exactly like my grandmother's chicken curry, he thought, and wandered in. At the time, Indian restaurants were almost all buffets, so Ashwin was intrigued. We struck up a conversation.

There were only two other people there that day, and Ashwin had time to kill. "Sit," I instructed him. I chose the dishes for him. I had a hunch I knew what Ashwin would like when he told me he'd recognized the scents. My hometown of Amritsar is less than 150 kilometres from Ludhiana, Ashwin's ancestral home. The cooking styles of the two Punjabi communities would have been almost identical.

Ashwin's father, Bhupendra, had been raised in Kenya, in the port city of Kisumu, but his own father sent him and his brothers to university in England. Three of them studied medicine, including Bhupendra. All three answered the call when Canada came looking for doctors. Bhupendra was a gifted internal surgeon who worked at the Calgary General Hospital.

They moved to Alberta after Ashwin's mom, Sushil, who was pregnant at the time, died from cancer. Ashwin was eighteen months old when she passed away. Bhupendra brought his parents, Faqir, also a doctor, and Pritam, with him to Calgary to help raise Ashwin, his only child.

The story unfolded over lunch. Ashwin stayed almost two hours. I kept bringing out more naan, more salad. We clicked on so many levels: I'm a passionate, creative guy, and I love music almost as much as I love food. We'd both had difficult relationships with our fathers. We've both butted heads with them.

Ashwin's father never recovered from Sushil's death. His love for medicine was like his son's love of music: all-encompassing. He'd travelled North America, lecturing on new techniques. On this, they could understand each other; most everything else was a challenge. Ashwin's dad battled alcoholism, which killed him in the end. He would die before Ashwin and his then-wife Sarah's firstborn, India, was born in 2002.

But perhaps the biggest similarity between us was the deep love and affection we feel for our grandfathers. We wanted to be just like them. We wanted to be successful to make them proud. Both were dead before they could see us achieve it.

Ashwin, who'd studied at the Musicians Institute, a private college in Los Angeles, told me he'd always wished his grandfather, Faqir, could have seen him make it. His dad grudgingly supported his son's career. But Faqir had always been deeply proud that after four generations of doctors, they had a musician in the family. I told Ashwin I'd wanted Vij's to be a place where my grandfather could come and chill, drink and enjoy life, and be proud of his grandson.

Ashwin is a deeply private guy, but by the end of that lunch he'd given me his phone number. And we started hanging out. I hadn't been in Vancouver very long, and I was so busy with the restaurant that I hadn't made many friends yet. Ashwin used to pick me up after I finished up for the night. We'd go out for two, three bottles of wine and talk for six hours about life. He was fascinated by my career, and I by his. He was touring a lot at the time, but whenever he was in Vancouver, we'd get together. He loved going out as much as I do. We're still that way. We love trying new restaurants together. These days, Ashwin is always trying to get me to the yoga studio; he's desperate for me to slow down. "You're one curry away from a heart attack," he'll scold me.

Meeru and I, after we married, used to visit him and Sarah at their places in Whistler, in Tofino. After twenty-five years, we've grown so close. We've gone through so much together. We both married headstrong women we worked with. We both struggled because of it.

I love him like a brother. We share everything. We know each other's darkest secrets. We are bonded for life. I have no energy for friendships. Everything I have, I give to my staff, to my restaurant. Ashwin is my one exception.

Around the time we met, I realized that I needed help at the restaurant. It was clear that I couldn't keep up. And we just kept getting busier. I was cooking, serving, handling dishes. It was a one-man show. But I'd keep getting stuck in the back washing dishes. Even if there was just one table seated, I wanted to be out front, warming up my customers and selling them on my food. So I decided to hire a part-time dishwasher during lunch hours, when Vij's was busiest.

I hired the first person to apply for the job, Amarjeet Gill, who was then thirty-two and had arrived in Canada five years earlier from Moga, in India's Punjab province. During the interview, I told Amarjeet that initially I might not have the hours she was looking for, but if she stuck with me through the first couple of months, I could eventually increase them to full-time.

She agreed. At first, she came in at eleven a.m. and left at two p.m., after helping tidy up. That's all I could afford. But I could tell that Amarjeet, who lived with her husband's family in Vancouver's Eastside, was having trouble making ends meet, and eventually she came to me: "Three hours just aren't enough," she explained. "I have a young family. I'm not earning enough." I told her that I understood, that I knew it was hard, and asked if she could please give it a bit longer. She agreed.

Within three months, she was working six days a week as our dishwasher/sous chef. This allowed me the freedom to create new dishes instead of spending all my time washing plates and chopping cilantro. Six months later, Amarjeet came to me again, politely asking if I could please consider limiting her work hours to five days a week.

Twenty-five years later, she's still with me, now as head cook and the general manager of all our kitchens. She's Meeru's hands, and the heart of the kitchen operation. It's impossible to separate what she and Meeru do. If Meeru is the creative and intelligent force, then Amarjeet taught her to manage with heart.

She instilled the ethos that we never fire anyone. If they're underperforming, we find them a job they're better suited for. In two and a half decades, we've only had to fire one person, for theft.

But her gentle, calm demeanour belies a tremendous power. When she believes something, whether it's a matter of staff salaries or the kitchen budget, she's unafraid to stand up to me. She's the only person in the organization, including Meeru, who I will listen to. Generally speaking, what Amarjeet says goes.

★

Meeru and I married on Christmas Eve, 1994, at a chain hotel in suburban Vancouver. It was about as glamorous as it sounds. December 24 was my only day off, and Meeru gamely agreed. Omi, her mom, laughed when she heard of our plans. It was all so outrageous. We barely knew each other. "Of all the men out there, you chose a waiter," Meeru's father, Shekhar, gently teased her.

The Richmond Radisson initially refused: "We don't do weddings on Christmas Eve," they told us. But I persisted. It was a tiny wedding, I pleaded. It was just Mama and Papa, Omi and Shekhar, and Meeru's two best friends. I didn't yet know many people in Vancouver.

My strict, traditional parents wanted a Hindu ceremony. Meeru and I didn't care either way. Her dad is an atheist, and when she and her sister, Ritu, were growing up, Omi didn't force them to go to temple with her. So we consented. Meeru wore a borrowed pink sari belonging to her cousin and tiny black sandals. I wore an Indian achkan, the traditional knee-length jacket.

Three days later, on December 27, we were back at work. Earlier that week, *The Georgia Straight*, the local alt weekly, hit news-stands with a glowing review of Vij's. Meeru watched as a lineup stretching an entire block formed outside the restaurant. We were running out of chicken. We were running out of lamb. She kept looking outside, and it just kept getting busier. That was the night she realized our little bistro was destined for greatness, she later told me. I was on top of the world, with a hopping restaurant and a beautiful bride.

For the first few months of our marriage, Meeru commuted between Vancouver and D.C. She had loose ends to tie up, and hurdles to clear with Canadian immigration officials. She moved to Vancouver permanently on February 5, 1995. She knew nothing about her new home. She could name the capital of every country on the planet, tell you who its president or prime minister was and any turmoil it had recently experienced. But of Canada, she knew almost nothing. Typical American. She couldn't even place Vancouver on a map.

Meeru had planned to find a job with a local nonprofit, but for the first four months she didn't have a work permit. She wasn't going to sit still alone in our apartment, though. She'd had a job since high school, when she worked at Bloomingdale's, and she hasn't stopped working since.

She didn't know a soul in this cold, rainy city, so she started hanging out in the kitchen with Amarjeet. Meeru spoke Hindi with an American accent. And since her parents spoke Punjabi to each other, she understood the language even if she couldn't speak it herself. Meanwhile, Amarjeet spoke only Punjabi but could understand Hindi, thanks to Bollywood movies. So that's how they conversed: Meeru spoke Hindi, and Amarjeet would reply in Punjabi. The two women who were to become the most important in my life were bonded by long hours and lots of laughter. These days they are tight as sisters, and finish each other's sentences.

Meeru's first job was handwashing in the three-section sink. She pulled on a pair of yellow rubber gloves one night and threw her elbows into the hot, sudsy water. As soon as she was done she started chopping onions, cutting herself as she learned. Her technique was poor, unlike anything ever taught in chef schools. But she didn't give a damn. She was happy where she was, doing what she was doing. None of those hang-ups bothered her. If anything, it freed her to be creative, to experiment without the fears that can inhibit professional chefs.

She remembered the smells of her childhood. She realized she could differentiate spices. From there, it was a very instinctive progression. She was a natural in the kitchen, and quickly found her feet. After five months she came to me and said, "Give me a chance to cook." "Of course," I said. Slowly, she became more and more creative, more assertive, and began experimenting with flavours and recipes. Over time, her role grew and grew. And as the business expanded, my administrative role did, too. Before long, Meeru was heading the kitchen and I was CEO of a fast-growing restaurant empire.

Meeru has a nose for spices. It's like accidentally getting pregnant and thinking, Fuck, I'm having a baby, but I don't actually want one—and then the baby is born, and you realize you're a fantastic mother. That's what happened with Meeru and food:

She'd never wanted it. But when the restaurant came into her life, it was like she was born to it.

She approached food from a very different angle than those of us professionally trained as chefs. There was no ego. In coming up with new recipes, Meeru would return to her grant-writing days. Back then, she'd have to focus on what made her organization, her project, stand out, why the United States Agency for International Development (USAID) should give them money over anyone else. She did the same thing with new recipes. She tried to make our food stand out, to make customers want to come to us rather than other Vancouver restaurants.

At first, we didn't know who our customers were going to be. Indians who came expected to eat food like my parents'. So Meeru made it about us: What did we want to eat? We began cooking for ourselves. We trusted our tastes and instincts. We knew that if we liked it, our guests would, too.

We used to close from two to five p.m. every day, to recharge. We'd take a long lunch and a nap. We were child-free, eating out all the time—never Indian, but everything else—and drinking wine by the gallon. I barely knew her. It was strange and wonderful. I'm not a natural reader, so Meeru knew my love was real when she saw me working my way through *The Economist* so that I could keep up with her.

We were busy, but we weren't making any money yet. Some days we cleared as little as $4. But we indulged where necessary: Meeru needed Sebastian Potion 9, a styling cream for her curly hair. And we drank only fine reds. By then, Meeru had also started to realize that I ate a lot, that I was actually chubby. With the ring on, I'd quickly let myself go. "You duped me with your fatness!" she once joked. I was guilty as charged.

Shortly after we married, our apartment in suburban Richmond was broken into and destroyed by thieves. In addition to the inconvenient commute to Vancouver, the theft had unsettled Meeru. We had what I thought was a casual discussion about moving into Vancouver, closer to the restaurant. She went and found a new apartment on Hemlock Street, within walking distance of Vij's, signing a lease without even telling me first. This was our very first argument.

I was furious. But when I yelled at her for not having consulted me—she could be as impulsive as my father, and it bothered me—Meeru immediately shut me down. "You do not yell at me like that," she said through clenched teeth. It was the first time I realized that I'd married my match.

★

People always ask why we have an all-female kitchen staff. It all comes down to the experience of one woman: Meeru's mom, Omi. Everything at Rangoli and Vij's is created and prepared by immigrant women with zero restaurant or chef experience. Few of them speak English. To Meeru, these are unbreakable rules. This is her way of giving women like Omi, who was deeply isolated by her move to the United States, the chance she never had.

In 1969, when Meeru was five, her father, Shekhar, an engineer, got a work visa for America. He'd been walking past the U.S. Embassy in Delhi one day and happened to see a banner poster urging Indians with science degrees to apply for U.S. visas. Shekhar planned to go first, to earn some money and find a suitable apartment, then bring Meeru and Omi. (Meeru's sister, Ritu, was born in the U.S.) But Omi was firm: "We all go, or no one goes." Omi didn't trust her husband alone. So all three got visas, and off they went.

They landed in Washington, D.C., in the middle of winter. Meeru was wrapped up in a massive chiffon scarf, which did little to protect against the cold. She was packed right off to the local public elementary school. And off Shekhar went to work. Their integration was immediate, deep, and lasting, the perfect mirror of Omi's experience.

Omi was then twenty-seven. She'd been torn from her mom, her siblings, the tight social circle that surrounds women in India. She spoke no English, and was further set apart by the bright saris and kurta pyjamas she preferred. The family couldn't afford English lessons for her. She didn't have a network in America. She didn't have any way to make friends. Even her children did not understand the depth of her struggles. There's a lot of fighting in the home when money is tight, when you can't understand the culture or the language that surrounds you, when you have few resources.

For a time, Omi found work at a fast-food restaurant, and then at Bloomingdale's as her English improved, but she started so late in life that she didn't enjoy it. Her co-workers saw her as an outsider.

Omi always felt alone in the U.S. She is an elegant woman who sang and cooked away her heartache, preparing elaborate, challenging meals for her husband and daughters. Growing up in Virginia, Meeru complained that she stank when she went to school. Before school, she used to drown herself in Love's Baby Soft perfume. But the curry odour that stuck to her jeans was "beautiful," she now recognizes—rich with love, emotion, complexity.

She sometimes saw her mom as a housewife, willing to waste her best years on afternoon soap operas. For role models and mentors, Meeru looked outside the family. She recognizes now that if someone had given Omi a chance at a career, her life might have been entirely different; she would have been empowered by the knowledge that she was really good at something, that she could earn money of her own.

With Amarjeet's help, Meeru started hiring women for the kitchen who were where her mother had been at twenty-seven. Her questions for potential hires are simple: Do you love to work hard? Do you love to cook? Do you love Indian spices? Her cooks must know spices; they must know how to cook a basic curry. If women have these qualities, Meeru knows she can train them. After all, she too learned to cook in a restaurant as an adult. Like Meeru, our kitchen staff are not professionally trained chefs. They're passionate cooks. That's enough.

It takes Meeru and Amarjeet roughly four months to train new staff and set a rhythm in our kitchens. Sometimes they hunt for new talent in Sikh temples. Everyone they've hired is originally from a village in the Punjab, and rarely speaks any English.

Meeru will tell you that hiring an entirely non-English-speaking kitchen staff is front-end heavy, with a learning curve for each woman to overcome, but we benefit in the long run. In the twenty-five years since we first opened Vij's, very few kitchen staff have left (unless it was for maternity leave, or if they'd left Vancouver). Over the years, our cooks have become our family.

In May 1998, Meeru and I brought Amarjeet to New York to help cook for the James Beard Foundation awards gala. Meeru and I booked two adjoining hotel suites. But when we got there, Amarjeet, who'd never travelled by herself before, told us she was scared to sleep alone in her room. So I ordered a cot for Meeru's and my room. "Just come sleep with us," I said. And she did.

Meeru and I share the same fundamental philosophy about the importance of food. Meeru's parents were not well off. They were refugees from a war who'd had to start over twice—first in India in 1947, then in the U.S. in 1969. The family didn't have money for extracurricular activities or braces for crooked teeth. The girls made do with two pairs of pants each. But one thing they never scrimped on was food. They spent weekends at farmers' markets long before these became popular destinations. Meeru never understood it back then; she was bored to death driving forty-five minutes to find the perfect tomato. But it instilled in her a love of food. At our restaurants, she works hard to build long-term relationships with local farmers and suppliers to source produce, seafood, and meats that align with our philosophy: to keep the flavours, spicing, and cooking techniques Indian, but to cook with ingredients that are locally available.

Meeru grew up knowing that no matter how hard and tumultuous life was for her immigrant parents, she was the apple of their eye. They let her know they'd left India to make a better life for her. And she'd sure as hell better do a good job of it. She's done a fucking brilliant job of it.

She sits on the board of the Vancouver Farmers Markets. Her baby, an annual international food festival at the UBC Farm called Joy of Feeding, brings together home cooks from different ethnic backgrounds to showcase their family's favourite comfort foods. The conceit is to highlight commonalities, to connect people through cooking.

Over time, Meeru's become increasingly concerned, and vocal, about global warming and climate change. She's the reason you'll find crickets on our menus; she advocates for insects as a healthy, sustainable protein source.

She ensures that our very limited seafood menu—halibut, sablefish, B.C. spot prawns, wild salmon, farmed char—is sustainably sourced. Our meats must be hormone-free and raised without anti-biotics. Our produce is farm-direct, sourced from nine local farmers.

One of our new dishes, Vij's Monarch Butterfly, is meant to draw attention to the plight of the endangered winged insects that migrate to Canada from Mexico every summer. It's made with wood ear mushrooms and slices of ghee-braised squash. The monarch's numbers have been decimated as a result of deforestation as well as the loss of milkweed, their primary food source, from herbicide spraying.

My obsession is water. I never allow water returned from the table to be dumped in the sinks. I collect water from jugs and half-empty glasses in big pails in the kitchen and use it to water plants outside.

It's an Indian thing. There, you'd never pour an unfinished glass of water down the drain. It's simply too precious. I'll never get used to the abundance of clean drinking water in Vancouver.

★

Omi also had a hand in our first big success: our bottomless chai. The idea for it was mine, but the creation was all Meeru's. She based her recipe on her mother's.

In December 1994, when we had one of our first big lineups, I ran to the kitchen to make chai for the waiting customers. I'd been appalled to see them lined up outside, standing in the rain, and wanted to find a way to apologize for the inconvenience and thank them for their patience. I thought holding something warm in their hands might help ward off the cold and encourage them to stay until I could seat them. We've always felt that generosity breeds generosity. It's the reason we give out free hors d'oeuvres to waiting customers and free naan with our meals.

The problem was, I was giving out muddy, bitter tea. If it cooks too long, chai—which simply means "spiced, milky tea"—will grow a sticky milk film on the surface. I'd thrown together milk, tea, cloves, and cinnamon and left it bubbling away on a cookstove in a closet in the back. The presentation was horrendous: It came out charred and darkened.

We needed to somehow keep it cooking away on the stove. We couldn't make a fresh batch every time a new customer walked in. There wasn't time, and we wanted to hand it to customers promptly. Since it would be their first experience at Vij's, it had to be perfect.

So Meeru pursed her lips and headed to the kitchen to figure out how to make chai that could simmer for hours at a time but remain delicate and retain its ochre colour, its balance of spices. It took two weeks to develop, but it was worth every second. As soon as I took my first sip I knew she'd nailed it. It was a massive hit, and helped launch us. Bear with me, and I'll teach you how she did it.

Growing up, Meeru's summers had been lonely. Her friends in suburban Washington spent the hot, humid summer months at the pool, at clubs, at camps. But her family didn't have money for these extravagances, so Meeru watched soaps with her mom: *All My Children, One Life to Live, General Hospital.* She can still recite the order. Shekhar, her father, was furious: "My daughter is going dumb from watching too many soap operas!" he would complain.

Omi could see that Meeru was bored, so one day she interrupted the soap marathon. "I want you to make my cup of chai today," she said. Now, Omi and her chai have a very special bond. She takes it piping hot, rich with fennel and cardamom, a little sweet, not too milky. Even when nothing else was going right for Omi, her chai had to be perfect. It was one thing she could control.

Meeru didn't even make it out of the kitchen with her first attempt. "No, that's not right," Omi said to her. "I can't see the steam—I need my chai hot. Tomorrow, my girl, it will be better."

But the next day Meeru didn't use enough cardamom. This went on for several more days until she'd perfected the spicing. "I need to see the steam rising from the cup. You need to first please my eyes," Omi told her daughter. "Then, as I bring the cup to my mouth, I need to smell the cardamom and the fennel, and my nose will tell me, Yes, she has the right spice mix. Almost automatically, my taste buds will be happy. Go—make me that perfect cup of chai."

So Meeru retreated to the kitchen, intent on making the perfect cup. She let the water boil and boil, but when she lifted the kettle off the stove, her unsteady ten-year-old hands somehow spilled the scalding water all over her belly. She was rushed to the ER with severe burns and spent the next fifteen days in bed.

When Meeru recovered, her father said, "Don't you dare take her back into the kitchen."

"I won't," Omi promised. That very afternoon, she asked Meeru, "Are you feeling better?"

"I'm fine, Mama," she said. "Then go back into the kitchen," Meeru instructed, "and make me the perfect cup of chai." And Meeru did.

Shortly after Meeru perfected our recipe in 1995 by gently tweaking her mom's, I hired a young woman, Seda Sim, to act as chaiwalla and hand out the tea to those lining up in the cold. It didn't cost much: just Seda's salary, and the tea, which ran us no more than a few cents a glass. But customers loved it.

In business, it is important to sweat the small stuff. Dreams can be realized by obsessing over the tiniest things.

★

Surprisingly, our next hit was also a liquid. We came up with the recipe for our famed ginger-lemon drink when we were still at the original location and didn't yet have a liquor licence. We didn't want to serve pop with our food.

Indians tend to drink still water with dinner. But we've found that North Americans tend to like something more. Coke is an awful pairing for Indian: It crashes against the heat on the tongue, intensifying the spice. It bursts your chest as you swallow.

So we developed a ginger-lemon drink as an alternative. It was inspired by an Indian street drink, numbu paani: masala lemonade, a favourite summer drink that's served ice-cold. I used to gulp it down in the afternoons when I was weak from the oppressive, forty-degree Bombay summer days. It mixes water, sugar, and fresh-squeezed lemon juice cut with a pinch of pungent black salt. It was the only thing that seemed to slake my thirst.

We added fresh ginger to give it a bit more punch and a hint of heat. (Some Indians spice the lemonade with cumin or saffron, even pepper.) We make ours with lemons, or limes if the former aren't juicy enough; the drink relies on the quality of the citrus. First we separate the juice from the pulp using a fine Japanese grater. Then we add fresh young ginger, sugar, mint, and carbonated water. It pairs perfectly with our food.

Before we put it on the menu, Meeru went to Ming Wo, the Granville Street kitchen store, and bought a set of beautiful green jars to serve it in. We bring a small carafe of carbonated water and a bowl of ice to the table, allowing customers to mix the lemonade themselves. It was an instant hit. Diners loved the ritual of mixing the drink to their taste.

Our next big hit was coconut curried vegetables: a lightly spiced dish made with a velvety, slightly sweet coconut milk. We'd wanted to create a dish for vegetarians that would rival our top meat curries. We'd found the coconut milk while poking around a Japanese store down the street. The coconut curried vegetables would become one of our most popular dishes.

For months we'd been getting stellar reviews when, one day, a car pulled up outside the restaurant and a staffer from *Vancouver Magazine* stepped out and announced that we'd won the "Best Asian" category for 1995 in the magazine's annual Restaurant Awards issue. It's a well-read issue, and a giant fucking deal. I was thrilled and deeply touched that the city had embraced the restaurant. For hours, I walked around on a cloud.

The following year, Vij's did not win. A wonderful Thai restaurant named Montri's took the honour, and we were overjoyed for Chef Montri Rattanaraj. But then I thought, Wait a minute, how do you compare Thai food to Indian food, or to Malaysian or Cambodian food? It seemed strange to lump "Asian" fare into one giant category when there was no "Best European" category. French and Italian cooking styles were rightly divided.

Meeru and I put together a letter gently explaining that the magazine's pan-Asian category, encompassing Indian, Malaysian, Vietnamese, Chinese, Sri Lankan, Singaporean, and other foods, was too broad, and perhaps a little offensive to the city's large Asian community. We felt that readers in a city as cosmopolitan and diverse as Vancouver deserved better.

The idea got through to the then editor-in-chief, Jim Sutherland. The following year, *Vancouver Magazine* introduced a host of new categories, including Best Indian, Best Thai, Best

Japanese, and so on. Restaurant owners, who become accustomed to getting their own way, tend to be brash and loud. But sometimes, by speaking softly, you can achieve better results.

Meanwhile, we kept getting busier. The chai helped. The ginger-lemon drink helped. Media acclaim helped. Meeru and I were a new couple, with a lot of energy to devote to our customers. We grew together as a couple alongside the restaurant.

I was still cold-calling reviewers and notable Vancouverites to try to get them to give us a try. But we had lineups by then. Meeru and I decided we needed a bigger space, so we moved a kitchen counter to the back in order to squeeze more tables into the cozy dining room, expanding from fourteen seats to twenty-one. Our friend Darryl Dugas, a hobby photographer, loaned us his beautiful shots of British Columbia wildlife. We repainted, installed new carpeting, and bought a new chalkboard. We were now able to put ten items on the menu. But still, the space was not big enough.

Plus, the little electric stove was creating headaches. It was a simple Kenmore kitchen stove, the kind you still see in residential homes. And it was always on the fritz, causing backups when there was already a lineup out the door. I'd be on my hands and knees, the curries slowly going cold, taping up a coil to get the elements working again. It was becoming impossible to continue there. I was serving tables and dreaming about what our restaurant might one day become.

A year and a half into Vij's, Meeru and I were walking home to our apartment on Hemlock Street. Down a back alley off Granville, we saw a shuttered Korean barbecue with a "For Lease" sign taped to the back door.

The realtor walked us through it the next day. She said it had been sitting empty for quite a while. I looked at Meeru as if to say,

Could this be the answer to our problems? She looked at me as if to say, We may be fucking nuts, but let's do it.

Inside, the restaurant was a complete disaster. The kitchen was flooded. The pipes had long since busted. Everywhere, there was stagnant water. As if to hammer home the point, a rat ran across the kitchen, deking puddles.

The Korean family had been living in the back, sleeping on a set of plywood bunk beds. The dining room had acted as the kids' after-hours playroom.

My job was to bargain with the realtor and sign a lease. The owner wanted $24 per square foot. I countered at $18. We met at $19.

By then, the lineups outside the restaurant stretched a half-block. We were clearing $600 a night on food alone in a twenty-seat restaurant. Those margins were unheard of at the time. I couldn't remember a night when we hadn't filled the room after six p.m. All I could think was, This stove has a proper hood. There's room to expand.

The relocation, which we began in mid-1996, was going to run us $50,000 we did not have. And Meeru was four months pregnant. We kept the first restaurant open almost until the last minute. I borrowed the money from Graham Webb, a regular who happened to be a contractor. Graham agreed to build the new space. It should have cost $110,000. He did it for half, and offered to let us pay him back slowly. I took the gamble.

Graham's demolition crew consisted of a man who lived on a boat on False Creek, a ferociously hard worker. For three months he slept in the old bunk beds at the back of the new Vij's location. He'd wake, work hard all day, then as the dust settled in the evening, he would go to sleep. When the dust got too bad he'd spend the night on his boat. Sometimes, he'd demand to be paid. He'd stop working until I paid him. I'd find $5000 and he'd get back to work for a week. Then he'd stop until I could put together another $2000.

It felt like a grand fucking adventure: We were going from twenty to fifty seats. I didn't know how to do any of it. But we figured it out, and God, we had fun. We chose the chairs, the colour scheme, and the paint by ourselves. I'd managed to pay off the $10,000 I'd borrowed to buy Café Arabia, but I hadn't saved any money. We were breaking even, travelling, eating out, drinking every night (at least until Meeru got pregnant). That's always been my problem: As soon as I have a little bit of money, I get comfortable, and I go out and spend it. Meeru's mom had given us a little money, enough for a down payment on a condo on East 10th Avenue, next to a beautiful old church. Everything was brand new, everything was fun.

We were still running a small little bistro together, sharing the workload. But we had a hunch that our lives would be overturned with the new restaurant. In August 1996, before we reopened, we sat down together in a loud coffeeshop at the corner of Broadway and Granville and decided to divide responsibilities clearly and evenly, according to our skill sets.

"You're charming everyone who walks through the door," Meeru said. "You should focus 150 percent on the floor." That's the moment when the front-of-house became my playing field. "The floor, the cooking shows, anything server- or customer-related is yours," Meeru added. She would manage payroll and kitchen staffing and would read, research, and trial new recipes.

We opened the new location in early September 1996. Meeru was seven months pregnant with our older daughter, Nanaki. A year earlier, when Meeru first brought up the idea of getting pregnant, I was hesitant. I wanted us to work hard, make successes of ourselves, then at forty go to India or Nepal and adopt two children. I didn't care whose body the babies came from, as long as they needed parents. By forty, I thought I would be established and financially secure. Meeru paused, listened to my reasoning, and a few days later, countered: "Give us three months to try to get pregnant. If we don't, we go your 'adoption at forty' route." She wanted to give it a biological shot. I was game to let fate decide.

My one cherished task at home was making Meeru's morning coffee. I took care in selecting the beans, grinding them fresh every day. Out of the blue one morning, she told me the coffee tasted "gross." I took it personally. The next day, I took great care in preparing it. Clearly unimpressed, Meeru asked if I'd brought home a new brand of beans. Pregnancy had not occurred to us because Meeru hadn't yet missed a period. Less than a month after our conversation about kids, fate had made a decision. Three years later, the morning Meeru's coffee tasted "gross" again, we knew immediately she was pregnant with Shanik.

I desperately wanted to make something of myself before fatherhood. But I came to understand that kids play an incalculable role in your happiness and success. I knew they would change me, which they did. For the better, it turned out.

Despite my apprehensions, I embraced parenthood. I was a mess when Nanaki was born in 1996. I'll never forget the rush of tears and joy I felt when I first touched her perfect, tiny fingers, saw her dark eyes peering up at me.

I adore my daughters. I love being in their company. I love watching them grow. Seeing Shanik's dimple spread across her left cheek after I've made her laugh gives me the same high as a climber must feel on summitting a new peak.

As they grew, they came to love spending time at the restaurant, which became a kind of playground; they'd bring in board games on school in-service days and would get spoiled rotten by the cooks.

★

At first, we kept both restaurants open. We couldn't afford to close the Broadway location to train staff at the new restaurant, which, in hindsight, was a big mistake. It meant that on opening night we didn't know how the restaurant would function. We just launched, with no systems in place. I was on the floor, running around like a madman. No one even knew the table numbers. It was like being thrown in a cold lake. We were all gasping for air, helplessly splashing around, trying to keep our heads above water. The service was terrible. The kitchen line was even worse. It's a miracle our regulars stuck with us.

But we were having fun. And we were busy. We would wake at eight a.m. six days a week and get to the restaurant every day by ten. Before that we had to do the Costco run to buy vegetables, produce. And before we opened we had to vacuum, set the tables, and clean the bathrooms. We worked like dogs until eleven and were home by midnight most nights after closing up.

When the girls were still breastfeeding, Meeru kept them at the restaurant. Later, we put them in daycare at UBC. Meeru would leave Vij's at five p.m. every day to bring the girls home. She'd spend every evening with them, from five to nine. One parent, we decided, had to be present to put them to bed, to raise them, really; and the other had to tend to the restaurant. We couldn't risk leaving Vij's alone for even an evening. If I got home before ten, I'd rush upstairs to tuck them in. There were many nights when I had to be content to peek in on their sleeping faces.

Sundays became my day with the girls: I'd cycle with them to Granville Island and spoil them with homemade fudge or an ice cream or a new toy. I was so busy that I was determined to make the time I did have for them perfect, exciting, fun.

Once, Meeru fainted and had to be taken to the ER. I was beside myself—not because my wife was in the ER; I knew Meeru was healthy—but because it was a Saturday, at four p.m., and I had to open the restaurant. What was I going to do with Nanaki? I actually asked hospital staff whether I could leave her with the nurses. It was a hospital, I figured: a safe space. Staff, and Meeru, looked at me like I was deranged. So without even phoning first, I took Nanaki to Amarjeet's house and practically hurled her onto the front porch for Amarjeet to catch.

I rarely got home before ten p.m., sometimes as late as eleven or twelve. I was exhausted. I'd need a drink as soon as I sat down. But no matter how late I was, Meeru and I made sure to sit down and eat a meal together. Even if it was midnight, Meeru was a firm believer in the importance of a family meal, in having empathy for the other person, showing interest in their day, an understanding that life is about more than just you.

We opened the new location in early September 1996. Meeru was seven months pregnant with Nanaki, our oldest daughter. It was busy, exhausting. But God we had fun.

NO RESERVATIONS

IT'S THE FAULT OF INDIANS THAT the world sees Indian cuisine as bland, homogenized, derivative. We have always served it cheap, and buffet style. Mom cooked. The daughters served drinks. By the cash register, a baby would sit idly gumming a discarded spoon. There were pink plastic tablecloths, loud Punjabi music, no stemware. Napkins were paper, bought in bulk. Wine, when it existed, came out of a box in the back. The meal ended with a handful of multicoloured anise- and fennel-flavoured sweets. This is how most North Americans experience Indian cuisine.

But this model never interested me. I never wanted to join the inane race among Indian restaurateurs for the best butter chicken. I've always wanted to elevate Indian cuisine, to give it the respect it deserves. It can and should be considered in the same category as French or Italian cuisine. So you'll never find butter chicken, or chicken tikka, or any of the bastardized derivatives of the Punjab's rich cooking at my restaurants.

I knew, of course, that change would not come easy. At first, people didn't get the food. Customers were thin on the ground. But I persisted. Slowly, people came around.

For starters, I completely reject the idea that Indian food should be searingly spicy and burn your mouth. All you're doing by cranking up the heat is masking flavours, subtleties. It's the same reason Molson and Coors encourage consumers to drink their beers ice-cold: this helps hide bitter, or dull flavours.

To catch the diners' attention, I knew we needed to come up with a dish to rival butter chicken. That was the impetus behind the lamb Popsicle, our signature dish at Vij's—still our most famous, and our most popular.

The idea for the dish came one night after a dinner party where friends had served rack of lamb. It was sublime. I knew immediately that I wanted to serve rack of lamb at the restaurant, but I didn't want anyone to pry the fine meat apart with a knife and fork. I wanted people to pick it up, to enjoy the meat's varied, beautiful flavours right off the bone. At the party, as we were eating the rack with our hands, someone commented that it looked like we were eating Popsicles made of meat. I just stared at him. It was an aha! moment. I thought if I called them "Lamb Popsicles" on the menu, people would know to pick them up with their hands. Meeru hated the name. But I convinced her.

I came up with a marinade for the rack of lamb and she came up with the fenugreek cream curry to pair with the turmeric spinach potatoes. I coached our customers on how to eat the lamb, how to enjoy it with their hands. "Do you make love with a knife and fork?" I would tease. The lamb Popsicles were a runaway hit, and became a phenomenon. We've never had anything come close to their success.

To make them, we marinate the lamb chops Mediterranean style, in Dijon and white wine, and finish them in curry. Each serving is grilled to order, not stewed en masse, Indian style. The lamb is served in a rich, creamy, garlicky fenugreek curry. Indian cooking traditionally involves yogurt, but I also like using cream, French style. As well, our kitchens use reductions, slow braises, and wines.

We are not fusion. At Vij's, we apply the rich Indian culinary traditions to new ideas, like local British Columbia goat, oven-braised then shredded into a kalonji curry, or ghee-braised beef short ribs in spicy cinnamon and red wine curry. To showcase B.C.'s terrific local seafood, like Dungeness crab, halibut, and sablefish, we'll create coconuty tomato-ginger curries to accentuate the flavours.

Western cuts of meat have only recently been introduced to Indian cuisine, and palates and attitudes toward meats, beef especially, are rapidly changing. In India, goat, lamb, and chicken are the meats of choice, as Hindus don't eat beef and Muslims don't eat pork. But we're cooking in Canada, and Indian cuisine is a natural fit for top Western cuts not often seen in India: beef and pork tenderloin, rack of lamb, beef short ribs.

For us, culinary finesse begins with fragrant spices. In our kitchens we add corners; we don't cut them. Rather than doing things faster, we slow it down. We hand-sift and roast and grind our spices ourselves. We could buy premixed masalas for a fraction of the cost and skip this tedious and labour-intensive step entirely. But we'd never consider it. The results are powerful spice blends of unusual clarity.

Visit Rangoli, our bistro, on the day cooks are roasting cumin on the stove, and you'll smell it all the way to Granville Street. They roast the spices in tiny batches on a small pan—just enough for the week. That's key. We don't want our spices sitting on a shelf. Their potency and flavour fade by the hour. We believe our customers can feel the love that goes into our cooking.

In the end, my goal in creating Vij's wasn't strictly financial. A cheap Indian buffet on Broadway offering tandoori chicken, butter chicken, aloo gobi, and a $6.95 Friday lunch special would surely have been successful and granted me a comfortable, easy life. But I've never wanted comfort. Money has never interested me. Change has motivated me. I wanted to bring awareness and respect to our cuisine and culture. I wanted to elevate the diverse cuisines of India to the realm of fine dining. I wanted people to look at and treat our cuisine the way they do French, Italian. I never wanted to be pigeonholed as "ethnic."

Look, the French have it easy: They take a clean, lily-white plate. They place two pieces of grilled broccoli off in one direction, a carrot in the other. Then they flash-grill a tiny bright red steak. They slice it thin as paper, then pour a little bright red jus to its left in the shape of an *S*. And voilà! It's beautiful!

It's very difficult to make Indian food pretty: It ranges from brown, browner, brownish. But what you can do with Indian food is serve it with love and passion and the utmost care. That's what we do at our restaurants.

Ours are also very modern restaurants. We focus on service, on ambience, on design, on communication with our staff and with our patrons. We are passionate restaurateurs who just happen to have an Indian restaurant.

We take great pride in the presentation of our food, keeping garnishes and ornamentation to a minimum and serving curries in or on simple, elegant bowls and plates. Our plates and bowls are still all handmade by local potters in a wide range of colours, shapes, and sizes, which we combine to showcase our curries.

Our service is fastidious. Tables are set with knife and fork crisscrossed over snow-white linen napkins. All plates and flatware are replaced between courses. Our wait staff silently wipe up spills and dribbles. Water is served in chilled, handmade copper ewers.

But it's also important to introduce the food in a way that isn't intimidating. That means meeting people halfway, describing menu items in relatable terms, coaching people to try popping an amuse bouche into their mouth whole. We'll explain a dish, and what wine to pair with it.

The key to surviving in this industry is thinking ahead and remaining focused on what you believe in. I've always said that in life, there are only two great unknowables: when death will take you and when a customer will happen to walk in. The only way to cope is to remain prepared for both. All that said, the truth is that, even after twenty-five years, we'll still get people calling up to ask, "But is there a buffet?" or "Why don't you serve butter chicken?"

★

Tom Cruise, Martha Stewart, and Goldie Hawn have more than one thing in common: They've all had to bide their time, to wait to get into Vij's. We have a strict first-come, first-served, no reservations policy. It doesn't matter how famous you are, how much you earn. There are no exceptions. When my parents come, they wait just like everyone else. This is not only the most democratic way; for me, it is the only way.

I have always sought to bring aspirational dining to a very egalitarian place. If a celebrity or a high-profile guest is staying at the Fairmont Pacific Rim in Vancouver's Coal Harbour neighbourhood, the concierge will typically get them the best table in the house at a restaurant of their choosing, forcing everyone else to wait. But never at my restaurants.

The lineups can take an hour, more often two, particularly after 2001, when *The New York Times* labelled us "easily one of the best Indian restaurants in the world." I remember our staff sitting around, dumbfounded, the day the *Times* ran their review of Vij's. That includes India, we kept saying. We had no idea what impact that one little line from Mark Bittman, the newspaper's food writer, would have. Robin Mines launched us and Mark Bittman authenticated us, on a global scale.

But I make sure no one goes hungry or thirsty while they wait. We offer complimentary hors d'oeuvres: pakoras, cassava root tossed in Indian spices, and papri chaat, a popular Punjabi street food made of fried dough and chickpeas, served with mint mango chutney and yogurt.

One Sunday in early 1999, a young man came into Vij's and spoke to our manager, Edward, asking if we took reservations for senior citizens. His father, who was visiting the city, was in poor health, and he really wanted him to experience Vij's before returning to Montreal. Edward apologized, explaining that no, we do not. He informed the young man that the best time to come in would be five-thirty. That way, he and his dad could snag a table without waiting. As the young man was leaving, he thanked Edward and said he would be back with his father, Pierre Trudeau, at five-thirty. Needless to say, Edward phoned me immediately.

By five thirty-five I was sweating: There was only one table left. The Trudeau family was then-mourning the loss of Michel, the youngest of Pierre Trudeau's three sons, who died in an avalanche while skiing in Kokanee Glacier Park, and I knew that the former prime minister wasn't doing well. This was the one and only time in my entire career that the idea of making someone wait for a table made me feel physically ill. Thankfully, the Trudeaus arrived, getting the last table. I served them personally. No customers dared try to speak to him (I made sure of it). They left the country's iconic former leader and his son alone for the night.

When it came time to leave, I walked him to the door, then I reached down to touch his feet. "Mr. Trudeau," I said, "I want to thank you for the policies you introduced in the 1960s to allow immigrants like me to come to this country and to make something of ourselves." He told me he'd never had Indian food so good, and wrapped an arm lightly around me.

When the late Robin Williams waited in line, he ended up giving an impromptu comedy show in the courtyard at Vij's. Harrison Ford became a regular during one of his semi-regular jaunts to Vancouver to shoot films. He used to come at our busiest time: eight p.m. on a Saturday night. He seemed to almost enjoy the waits, the normalcy of it.

Tom Cruise and Katie Holmes, Mark Zuckerberg, Gwyneth Paltrow, none of them have ever kicked up a fuss about the wait. In fact, we've noticed over the years that the bigger the star, the less they tend to care. It's the up-and-comers, the entitled young actors and pop stars with something to prove, who tend to be pushier, who ask our hostesses whether they "know who I am." (Generally, they do.)

I must remind you here that I grew up in India and my movie stars all come from Bollywood. Tom Cruise aside, I have never recognized a single one. I would call up Meeru in the middle of service to ask, "Who is Zach Galifianakis?" or, "What is this *Twilight* movie?" While my front staff were always excited by a celebrity appearance, the kitchen staff were as clueless as I was. When they asked about the buzz, I would explain, "One of their big stars is in for dinner." Now, the day Bollywood star Akshay Kumar came into Vij's, the tables turned: the kitchen staff and I were so excited by Kumar's presence we could barely focus.

The seating policy was implemented from the get-go, and it remains one of my favourite aspects of the restaurant. It allows all concerned to be on an equal level, one to the other. The policy was inspired by Mahatma Gandhi's teachings.

"All men are brothers," Gandhi wrote. "I have known no distinction between relatives and strangers, countrymen and foreigners, white and coloured, Hindus and Indians of other faiths." I have always followed that philosophy. The welfare of all, sarvodaya, he said, should be our aim.

Gandhi had a huge influence on me when I was growing up, and it's important for me to live by his philosophy. He single-handedly changed the course of a nation, ridding India of an empire using nonviolent means. He did it all out of a love for country, wearing nothing but a loin cloth.

Who cares how much money you have, where you were educated? Not me. Whether you are a teacher, a doctor, an actor, in our restaurant you will be treated with the same love and respect. I believe there is something sacred in everyone. Above all, I believe we are equals.

Customers either love the wait or they hate it. Our hostess will always inform you of the wait time when greeting you, and inquire whether you're sure you're interested in waiting. John Legend, the musician, stormed off when I told him of the wait.

In the end, I've never treated our restaurants as businesses. To me, they are extensions of my own home. We treat people the same way we would if they'd come to our place for dinner: You have come to my home, and I'm going to take care of you. That is why it is called Vij's, not the Taj Mahal.

★

Mike Bernardo, our director of operations, joined us in 2002, originally as a manager and wine director. The London, Ontario, native had moved to B.C. at eighteen, after high school, lured by the mountains—he loved to snowboard. He later left for Europe and spent four years working at the Balmoral, the iconic five-star Edinburgh hotel, which sits above the Waverley train station at the heart of the Scottish capital's downtown.

When I first hired Mike, fifteen years ago, he was twenty-five and trying to work his way out of the industry, teaching scuba diving, wakeboarding, surfing, and kayaking on Vancouver Island, trying to break into ecotourism and guiding. I was looking for a manager at Vij's, and a friend of his, one of our former managers, suggested I speak to him. Mike was intrigued by the opportunity to manage a restaurant on his own, and came to Vancouver for an interview.

I took immediately to him. I saw in him the same drive, passion as I have. After our initial interview Meeru was a bit skeptical: Mike knew nothing of Indian food, and came across as a bit of a "surfer dude." "Trust me," I told her. "He'll be an amazing fit." I was right. We sometimes joke that Mike is Meeru's second husband, and my first. Simply put, we love him.

Not only did Mike not know anything about Indian food, he'd never heard of Vij's—he was frank and honest about that. He struggled to remember all the names of the curries on the menu.

But his humble approach and his wisdom were immediately apparent. We hired him for the role of general manager, but for the first month he was a busser. Then over the next few months he worked his way up through every other position in our team system. Only when he knew every position first-hand and had tasted everything on the menu and understood our curries did he take on the managerial role. Not once did he ever worry that he wouldn't carry the authority of GM, even though his own staff were schooling him.

He was deeply committed. In his first year with us, Mike had a major car accident. Still, he came in the very next day, and continued working only to realize a week later that his shoulder was broken and required major surgery.

Mike was replacing a very popular manager, Karla Welch (then Kulos), who was raised in Powell River, B.C. She'd first joined us as a server. "I've wanted to work for you for a long, long time," she told me when we first met. "I want to learn everything I can from you, and eventually become your manager." Karla was phenomenally driven, and did in fact become our manager. She might still be with us had she not served a customer visiting from Los Angeles named Matthew Welch.

A week later, Matthew wrote Karla a letter from California. He'd felt a connection, he said. If she'd felt the same, he asked her to write back. Karla later flew to L.A., where they spent five days together. Their relationship followed the same essential blueprint as mine and Meeru's: It was love at first sight, two separate cities, a shared confidence in a gut feeling that things would work out. Within a few months, Karla left to move to L.A. and marry Matthew. He was an established photographer for major Hollywood stars. She joined him as a stylist, in much the same way that Meeru started dishwashing for me. Today, Karla has become one of Hollywood's biggest stylists, with a client list that includes Justin Bieber, Michelle Williams, and Felicity Jones. I'm incredibly proud of her. And I felt reassured that I wasn't a total asshole when Karla, after becoming a big success in L.A., told me that everything she'd learned about working hard and focusing obsessively on details came from me.

But let's get back to Mike. While in Edinburgh he'd also worked for a year at a Michelin-starred restaurant, The Atrium, where the owners had allowed him to apprentice with their sommelier as a junior wine buyer, attending tastings and learning the trade. He loved serving, the vibrancy of the floor, but wine had become his joy and passion. So Mike trained as a sommelier, earning his certificate.

Because he'd apprenticed at one of Europe's top hotels, I trusted him innately. He knew that at Vij's he could marry server and sommelier, with the goal of taking over our—admittedly then pathetic—wine program.

Meeru and I drink wine almost every night, and I'm now a certified sommelier. Back then, though, our wine list consisted of five whites, five reds, one rosé. They were all listed at the same price. You could buy by the glass or bottle.

But I kept a secret stash in the back, for connoisseurs. When they arrived I'd haul out my private selection of five top bottles they could choose from. But at heart, I always want my restaurants to be democratic institutions, and when you're treating certain customers in a different way, you're not staying true to that vision. So Mike came in at the perfect moment, first adding a single page of reds, whites, some sparkling wines.

Mike, by then, had come to know Indian food as well as any Indian gourmet. He'll tell you nothing pairs better with Indian food than champagne. It's got great acid and a full structure to it. The bubbles and carbonation serve to cut through the rich flavour- ing, cleansing your palate with every sip. It's a powerful drink, the only one that can truly stand up to the spices.

Slowly, under Mike's guidance, the wine list grew to two pages, then gradually to a full book. Back then, B.C. laws barred restaurants from having spirits, save for a few liqueurs. But when laws were relaxed, allowing us to serve hard alcohol, we began offering four cocktails that paired nicely with the spicing and fla- vours inherent in the food.

With a white, Mike will say you want to either balance the dish or provide some contrast to it. I usually suggest a white Rhône: It's got a fuller body. It's not oaky, so it balances the rich, full body of the curry and can still stand on its own. Or, if someone prefers an even fuller bodied white, I'll find one lean and crisp, with a mineral, flinty style that can relieve the richness of the food. But I'd never let my customers drink a really big oaked wine or one with rich, buttery flavours typical of certain types of Chardonnay. These wines set up the same burning sensation as spicy dishes, and will accentuate their heat. But don't avoid Chardonnays altogether. Those with a tropical fruit note or a Chablis style work really well with our dishes.

There are so many wines that pair well with our fare, but reds are far trickier. And it's especially tricky in this era of climate change. These days, it's almost impossible to find a good low-alcohol—11.5 or 12 percent—red. The summer growing season has become so incredibly hot that it increases the sugars in the fruit (which cre- ates the alcohol). And the alcohol does the same thing as the tannin:

It dials up the chili flavour, the heat component, drowning out the more subtle flavours.

For a red, one with big tannins, or a giant, heavy Cabernet, will bring more heat with every sip. Five bites into your meal and there'll be no flavour profile, just substance and heat. The key is to choose a fruit-forward, low-alcohol, low-tannin wine, one that starts out with plum or tart berry flavours when you first sip it.

Mike is forty now. His major strength is first and foremost wine. But he's grown up in the industry, and after fifteen years with us, he knows our business intimately. Over the years his role has grown to director of operations and wine director at Vij's. He's the point of entry when it comes to anything relating to the front of the house.

He also brings a lot of experience to the development side of things. He knows what the floor should be like; he can spot operational inefficiencies. He's a great manager. Our employees adore him. He's laid-back, approachable, but never soft. And he cares deeply for them. He's often the buffer between me and the front staff when they make even a small mistake like not refilling a water glass as they walk by a table. Over the years, Mike and I have had some serious fights. But he has involved himself in the company through loyalty, hard work, and his devotion to our staff.

Mike is Meeru's front-of-house equivalent: She runs the kitchen. He runs the front. The ethos that guides their treatment of staff is remarkably similar, and our engines hum because of it. My job is to bring these various pillars together.

Mike has since opened his own bistro under the Vij's umbrella: the twenty-four-seat Vij's Sutra, at Victoria's Public Market in the historic Hudson's Bay building downtown. He spends four or five days in Victoria every month overseeing Sutra, which he launched in 2014.

We trust our staff to speak their minds. It's a relationship built on mutual respect. If they show chutzpah and drive and work ethic, we offer many opportunities. When Mike and Laura, a former Vij's employee, showed an interest in a factory we later built in Cloverdale, B.C., to mass-produce our frozen line, we allowed them to design the layout for it. We gambled that their inexperience would be out-weighed by their drive. And we were right.

There is no hierarchy among our staff. We work together under what I call the "team system." At most restaurants, rigid staffing pyramids rule: They tend to be run like armies, where a sergeant could never address a general. I don't subscribe to that bullshit. We are a team of equals, from maître d', to food runner, to manager—we all work together to make the night a success. And at the end of it, tips are pooled and equally shared. That tipping practice also puts us at odds with the standard practice at most top restaurants.

In our restaurants there are no staff washrooms, no staff meals. There is no staff dining room. We all hang out and eat together. The concept is simple: You respect me, I'll respect you. In our kitchens, there are no sous chefs, no sauciers, no chefs de partie. They're all cooks. We are relentlessly egalitarian, an environment we have created ourselves; it marks a radical break from the running of most fine restaurants. And we like it that way.

That said, I have serious anger issues. And I like things done a certain way. When someone argues back, I fight. I get worked up when things aren't just so. When I walk into the kitchen, I can feel the atmosphere shift as my staff tense up. I'll ask, "Why is the oven hood so dirty?" "Why is that cilantro in the garbage?" "Why is that pot just sitting there?" When it comes to my restaurants, I'm a per- fectionist. My car can be a disaster, but my kitchens must be spotless. I'm fastidious at work, and demand nothing less of my staff. When the kitchen is untidy, I get angry. "Clean the fucking thing," I've been known to yell. Sometimes I feel I'm constantly barking orders.

That was the way I apprenticed. It was demeaning. It was dif- ficult. I was a grown man, educated at a top European hospitality school, and I had to take shit from chefs like a twelve-year-old. Kitchens are full of testosterone. There's a lot of yelling and fight- ing and pot throwing.

Meeru, however, would walk into the kitchen, no matter its disarray, and empathize with how busy the previous night had been. She would say, "Hi everyone" and "How are you, Amarjeet?" and ask the women about their day, their children. It would take her a half-hour before she'd get around to getting them to organize it and clean up. "We're all ready to go by five-thirty, no matter what," she reasons. "So why bother with the negative energy?"

Meeru has never raised her voice at work (though at home she raises it plenty), and it angered her when I did. Meeru has never had onions thrown at her by chefs. I think that's what it all boils down to. She's never seen a chef slam an oven door so hard the glass broke. She won't tolerate the stress, the bravado, the bragga- docio typical of most kitchens. In our shops she demands calm, Zen. This she takes very seriously. Meeru's rationale is "We have no right to ruin other people's days." While I appreciate this rationale on paper, to practise it in real life—not just for me, but for many of our other front staff—isn't always easy.

At home, Meeru and I got into some pretty ferocious fights about work. My debating skills are no match for her intellectual

might: She'll dance from one point to the next, deking my argu-
ments, dodging when I happen to land a solid point. But through
it all, we held steadfast to the rule that we never go to bed angry.
For sixteen years, we stuck by that rule.

Meeru describes her job as "cheerleader," ensuring that everyone
is okay, that the kitchens are humming along, focused under pressure.

She spends half her day at Rangoli and the other half at Vij's,
overseeing the kitchens. Amarjeet is our kitchen manager at Vij's.
Rajwinder Samra is our kitchen manager at Rangoli. Sarbjit Randhawa
manages the factory, Vij's Inspired Indian Cuisine. All three women
started off with us with no English and no work experience. I remember the day many, many years ago when Meeru came home and told
me that her new dishwasher had come to her and said that she'd
had great dreams as a schoolgirl in India and that those dreams took
a detour when she was arranged to marry a boy from Surrey, B.C.,
at the age of eighteen. Now she was twenty, with a newborn. "I need
your help," she told Meeru. "I want to become more than a dishwasher.
I know I'm smart. And I want to make something of myself." That
twenty-year-old is Sarbjit Randhawa, who now manages our factory.

Meeru will cook new recipes with Amarjeet three times. Once
she has the recipes down pat, it's her job to teach the other cooks.
They cook from memory, not recipe.

Meeru and Amarjeet run the kitchen like a sisterhood. They
talk, they have fun, they are creative. They play around with recipes, tweaking them, modernizing them.

None are trained chefs: They cook by smell, not by rote, and
can tell when something needs more cumin, more coriander, more
tomato, more salt. Except for Meeru, almost all are vegetarian. And
none have tasted our meat dishes.

The cooks choose one of two shifts: The first runs from six a.m. to two p.m., the second from three p.m. to closing. Most carpool, arriving together, taking turns behind the wheel. Twice per shift, one, generally the newest cook, will make chai, which they drink standing up. It's far sweeter and milkier than the tea we serve at Vij's. Ours is "city tea." Theirs is what we call Punjabi village chai.

None of them will ever have to hire a shrink: They are each other's psychiatrists. They talk all day—about their kids, their husbands, what they did the night before. Whenever one has a problem, it's shared, analyzed, endlessly discussed. Every time I walk into the kitchen, I hear laughter. Ours is a busy workplace, but a happy one.

Culturally, for our cooks, marriage is not optional but rather a given, and like 95 percent of Indian marriages, theirs are arranged. They get six weeks off for their weddings, which are conducted in India. If they need more time to get to know their new husband and his family, they phone Amarjeet, who always gives them an extra two weeks' holiday. She knows this is the last time the women will see their husbands for three years. Changes to the immigration system have slowed a process that used to take six months. They support each other through the tough waiting period. Each of them has had to endure it—me included. We understand the pain, the frustration.

When they have a problem, personal or financial, they'll often come to Amarjeet or to Meeru and me; we'll do whatever we can to help them. Always, we speak Punjabi. Oğuz Istif, our brilliant, Turkish-raised chief financial officer, whom they adore, will always greet them with the traditional Punjabi blessing, "Sat Sri Akal." They can't resist Oğuz, with his deep, soulful eyes and impeccable manners, and make sure to set food aside for him.

We all go through hard times. At some point or another, we all hurt. We all need a helping hand. When I'm down, feeling so stressed out, overstretched—financially and otherwise—my staff have stepped up to help me through it. "Keep focused," they'll say. "We've got you."

History has taught us that in war, morale is the single greatest factor to success. Troops with high morale can succeed against immense odds. Business is just another battlefield. Morale is just as crucial in a workplace.

★

If only my relationship with my parents ran as smoothly as our kitchens. In 1996, two years after we married, we asked my father to run the old restaurant, at 1453 Broadway. We'd renamed it Manny's Lunch in honour of Manmohan, my father. By then, my parents had immigrated permanently to Vancouver to join Meeru and me.

Papa had always wanted to run a restaurant. For him, Manny's was a dream come true. We hung a new neon sign above the sidewalk and hired a cook and a manager. Manny's did well during lunch, but my dad would close at four p.m., and we soon realized that it couldn't survive on lunch alone. But the problem wasn't just revenue.

My father is a great salesperson, a natural charmer, the type to gently spoon chutney onto his customers' plates. But he'd never served professionally, and his business experience was all in India, where he was used to screaming at underlings who'd scurry about like rats, obeying his every command. That style got him nowhere with his Canadian staff, who would roll their eyes or giggle at his outbursts.

At heart, his problems with his daughter-in-law were no different: old-world styles clashing with more modern attitudes. His relationship with Meeru was doomed from the start. I understand that now. And it helps take away some of the sting. For me, it was an intensely stressful time: My parents and my beautiful new bride could not seem to get along.

Meeru is American-raised, modern, emotional. She doesn't take shit from anyone, and she refuses to subscribe to the old-school dictates and traditions. She's no bahu: the obedient, timid, hard-working, stereotypical Indian daughter-in-law who leaps up to prepare food for her in-laws the minute they walk through the door. Nor is my mother some sari-clad battle-axe. But my dad believed that, as Indian parents, they could expect a degree of solicitude from Meeru similar to what his parents required of Mama.

Meeru speaks her mind. She can be judgmental, quick to lash out. "You can't control your own wife," Papa would say. In the beginning, I'd try to calm Meeru, to get her to see that she was being quick to rise. As an Indian son, it was deeply disrespectful for me to side with Meeru. But what I felt, more than anything, was caught between them.

Fundamentally, Meeru was right: "This isn't India!" she'd say when I'd raise the subject. "We live here now." And yet my parents were also not wrong. In the end, I don't really blame either of them. Each came armed with expectations based on their unique heritage, their upbringing.

Sometimes Meeru overreacted. And she occasionally imagined wrongs that never existed. She could have backed off. She did the opposite. Meeru's brashness, her confidence—that's what I fell in love with. But with my parents that spitfire sensibility worked against her.

Meeru always got on well with Mama, who is softer, more innocent than my dad. But culturally, they were so different. Meeru understood: Mama is a devoted, traditional wife. She follows the old traditions. But she wanted none of it. Hearing Meeru ordering her son to feed the baby, to do the dishes and tidy up, came as a shock to my mom.

I could sense the relationship going south the first time they spent any time together, in 1995, shortly after we married.

Things got off to a rocky start. My parents arrived at the crack of dawn one fall morning, fresh from India and full of Indian parental expectations. Meeru was then nine months pregnant. All she could think about was her lower back pain and lack of sleep. She refused to play the role of doting daughter-in-law. I found myself torn between them.

On their fifth day in Vancouver, my parents grew furious when Meeru left to visit friends. To me, they complained that she'd abandoned them, leaving them with nothing to eat. There was plenty of food, as Meeru had made clear. They could have made some rice and warmed up one of the curries in the fridge. But in their generation, that was not done. They wanted their daughter-in-law to prepare and warm the meal and to sit down with them. That was the respectful thing to do.

An empty mind is the devil's workshop, I firmly believe. Your mind goes crazy when you're sitting around all day; you obsess over silly, imagined slights. "She didn't offer me a second cup of chai," my father would complain.

They never sat down with Meeru and explained that they felt hurt. They only complained to me. I would then tell Meeru, and she'd ask why they wouldn't just speak to her about it. If she had approached them, they would have mistaken her once again as having a brazen attitude toward them. I became the go-between. I heard it from both sides: "How could you treat us this way?" Papa would ask. "Why can't you stand up for your wife?" Meeru wanted to know.

My parents stayed with us for only two weeks. And that was enough to create a big enough tear in the familial fabric that no seamstress could mend. My parents, who'd wanted to finally live with the son they had invested so much in, moved a few blocks from us. At one point, they suggested living together as a joint family. "No way," Meeru said simply, finally. Frankly, even I couldn't imagine living with my parents and my father's unending questions: Where were you last night? Were you stumbling when you came in? Were you smoking?

For a while, there were no fights. We never discussed it. But there it was: this icy, unspoken anger.

Vij's, meanwhile, was endlessly busy. And since I was working around the clock and had a new baby at home, I couldn't see my parents often to try to smooth things over. I'd come home late at night. I'd eat an entire brick of brie and drink a bottle of wine to myself. I put on weight. Instead of getting angry with me over my late-night snacking, Papa would yell at Meeru. In his mind, Meeru was refusing to censure or stop me. My ill health, my weight gain, was somehow her fault.

"Has your son ever listened to anyone?" Meeru would reply. "I'm not the one giving him food when he raids the fridge, drink in hand." "But it's your responsibility," Papa would say. "Look at his belly: Why aren't you telling him not to eat cheese, not to drink late at night?" "Why the hell is this my fault?" she'd respond. I can't believe Papa would think anyone could control or change me, but there he was, picking away at her for my growing belly.

The more they fought, the more I wanted to get the hell away from them all. At the time, I was busy building the restaurant, juggling my role at home, as son, as husband. It was exhausting. I'd never wanted a life like this. I'd wanted a relationship between my wife and parents. When we first met, Meeru and I were constantly doing things together. I'd come home, we'd drink and make love. We were so happy. I couldn't figure out how to get back there.

Perhaps because Meeru looked Indian they expected her to behave like an Indian. But it was effectively an intercultural marriage between an Indian and an American. Growing up, Meeru had never felt the typical Indian pressure of trying to please her mom and dad. She didn't have time for what she calls the "Indian Boy Syndrome," a reflection of the culture's obsession with boys, and would roll her eyes at my parents' unwieldy devotion.

And yet it was always Meeru who was first to call Mama on her birthday. She'd embrace my father whenever she saw him. She never told my father off, would never call him an asshole. They are her children's grandparents, and she only ever treated them with respect.

Then one morning in the winter of 1997, Papa called me. He'd fallen on the ice. Meeru and I were overwhelmingly busy (she'd returned to work at the restaurant when Nanaki was three months old), so I told him he should visit his doctor to make sure he was okay. Our response clearly enraged him. From his perspective it became, You abandoned your father, who was sick and in pain.

He never went to the doctor. When he did, two weeks later, he was told that his lungs had filled with liquid and needed to be drained. It was a day operation, and didn't require an overnight stay.

When I got to the hospital, he was furious. Lying in his narrow little bed, he looked up at me and said, "Rajdeep has kept your sister under control. And I've kept your mother under control. But look at you, you can't even control your own wife. At the end of the day you're nothing but a henpecked husband. My own son!"

"Hush now," my mother said, trying to stop the fight.

It was ridiculous, but he was right about one thing: He controls the woman in his life. While he adores my mother he has exerted his firm will over her. It's something Meeru recognized early, and deeply resented. She and my father were like two poles planted side by side—never would they meet. It's not like I was looking for perfect harmony. I just didn't want to deal with the bickering.

As for me, I was hurt by his words and his tone, but I shrugged it all off. My anger with my father quickly fades. We always make up. Two hours would go by, and I'd forget why we'd been fighting in the first place. My father and I are devoted to each other, and love each other deeply. I've never had a falling out with him that lasted more than a day.

In his mind, Papa had toiled away for years for me, spent a chunk of his retirement savings, took out loans, all to send me abroad, to ensure that I could reach my destination. In his mind, he'd given up his own happiness for me. He'd left India to help me. He'd even given up hope of coming to live with us, as is expected of Indian children. In his mind, he was a great person for having done all this, and on his stooped shoulders I was standing tall. That I might reach unimaginable heights would all be due to him, to his immense sacrifices. And in a way, all this is true. He did guide me to the right path. To an extent, the values he instilled in me did shape the person I have become. And he certainly sacrificed to send me to Austria to study.

But there was one fight where I wish I'd chosen my words and actions differently. In Indian culture, a son traditionally gives his mother a monthly salary, a token amount, generally under $500. It hadn't occurred to me that my mother might want it, but my father said to me one day: "I think you should give Mama some money."

"Why?" Meeru asked when I raised it with her. "If they need the monthly stipend, I'm okay with giving it; but we just had a baby and have barely started earning money for ourselves." When I explained the gift's cultural origins, she quipped rudely, "No, this is your dad's Indian culture. This token Indian shit, I'm not doing it." To Meeru, these traditions appear dated and bizarre. In the end, I sided with her. While she's perhaps not wrong, the joy that this act of love and respect would have given my parents still upsets me. In hindsight, I wish I had insisted on giving it. The relationship was already rocky. The last thing it needed was another fissure.

At Manny's Lunch, meanwhile, things had continued to deteriorate. My father felt that if he was helping serve, tips should be divided, and he should be allowed to keep his share. I knew that no one would consent to working just three hours a day and have to share their tips. I tried to explain that he was earning a good salary, and that if he forced his staff to divvy up tips none would continue working for him.

Meeru, who was acting as a referee between my father and his staff, was getting increasingly frustrated. She was bitching to me behind my dad's back while my dad was bitching to me behind hers. I was just trying to run my restaurant and find some kind of peace. But no one was letting me.

I couldn't seem to find the words to ask him to calm down, to back down. When I did try to speak to him he, rightly, screamed at me that he'd been in business his entire life.

This pattern persists even today between my father and me: What begins as a slight skirmish quickly explodes into a huge fight that ends with him telling me I can't control my wife and me telling him she doesn't need to be under my control. It's exhausting.

One day, Papa called up Meeru: "I refuse to work here anymore," he said. "I'm done. I don't get any respect." He was still furious about the tips.

Later, when he'd calmed down, he called me and said, "I'll come back." But this time I put my foot down. I said, "No, Papa: You're done now. I'm relieving you of your responsibilities." And I meant it. I stuck to my ground.

He was so hurt. He lashed out, blaming Meeru. He believed the decision must have been hers.

But Meeru had nothing to do with it. I was tired. I'd had enough of the petty fighting. I had a child of my own, a new restaurant earning $15,000 a month, bills to pay, a business to build.

Still, it was devastating. I'd fired my own father. He was sixty-seven years old. I gave the job to someone else. I did it to save my family, to save myself. I knew we could never continue in this way.

But I've never forgiven myself. It is my biggest regret as a son. I believe that work keeps you young. And in the years ahead Papa's health faltered. Had I allowed him to keep working, I believe he might not have faced all the health issues he has. He might not have so quickly gone downhill. Those thoughts haunt me. They keep me awake at night. But at the time, I was so angry I didn't even help him fill out job applications.

Later, I came to understand that my father's driving purpose was to give me a good life. Rather than judge what he did, I should have worked harder to understand why he was doing it. At the time, I did not.

Almost everything in our restaurants is made locally and by hand: our plates and bowls, lamps, tables, and even the bar.

RANGOLI

BY 2003, VIJ'S WAS BUSIER THAN we could handle. And our customers were getting frustrated: When the craving struck for
Indian food, they had no choice but to line up for a table at Vij's.

We'd also noticed that we'd begun losing some of our clientele—
students and young couples—as our menu prices began inching
upward. Meeru had by then become a full-fledged Indian culinary
artist. (Note: These are her words, not mine! With a cheeky smile, she
asked me to use them.) She'd begun creating complex, original recipes.
Each menu item was taking hours to prepare, and we'd had to hire
many more staff to assist. We could never open Vij's for lunch, a constant complaint, because our cooks began prepping dinner at six a.m.;
we could not handle a second meal. And everything we were using in
preparing these dishes was local and sustainably sourced, none of it
cheap. All this meant that our menu prices had to be increased.

Expansion, to meet growing demand, was the logical next
step. But before we could begin scouring the city looking for a
second locale, an opportunity opened up next door.

The City of Vancouver had been digging up the streetfront, hurting Vij's West 11th Avenue neighbour, Max's Deli, which relied partly on walk-ins. It was water-main work, and after two months I figured that the owner, Bruce Redpath, would be frustrated. Meeru and I decided that I'd go talk to him and offer to buy out his lease. It turned out to be our one and only conversation: I inked a deal with Bruce that day, and wrote him a cheque for $110,000.

It made perfect sense. We needed to grow. We knew the location worked. And we knew Vij's would help draw warm bodies to the new place. The only hitch was what to do with it. We had a prime spot, but no solid concept for it yet. In a way, it was like having a blank canvas. Thankfully, I'd arranged to transfer ownership two months from the purchase date, giving us a bit of time to work on the concept. Rather than just knocking out the wall dividing the two spaces, we wanted to do something entirely new.

"We have two months," I told Meeru, Mike, and Tara Burke, then a server at Vij's. "What do we want to do?"

Casual Indian in a bistro setting, we quickly decided. That way, we could serve lunch and offer a slightly lower price point on dinner to attract new customers, and keep our younger clientele. And Meeru and I realized that it could also function as a mini-market for a line of packaged, gourmet take-home foods—an idea we'd been quietly batting around for a few years. I'd known the concept was a good one; I'd just needed to do the right marketing to make sure people knew about it. This beautiful new restaurant could provide just that.

The packaged meals had been inspired by Omi, Meeru's mother. Meeru had had a terrible delivery with our second daughter, Shanik. For the first six weeks after the birth she couldn't walk or even stand, and poor Shanik had been born with a skull fracture. Omi stayed with us for the first month and a half, helping out with the cooking and with Nanaki, who, at two and a half, was sweet, fun, and more than a bit jealous of her newborn baby sister. (When Shanik cried, she'd ask Meeru to "send the baby back to April 23rd," the day Shanik was born.) Before Omi left, she cooked a dozen masala curries, freezing them in labelled Ziploc bags, enough for two weeks.

We were exhausted. Meeru was up all night with Shanik and tending to Nanaki, who was out of diapers but still getting potty trained. And with Meeru home with the girls I was working around the clock, running Vij's on my own.

Omi's frozen bags were a godsend: All we had to do was cook a bit of rice and add a bit of either chicken or vegetables to her prepared masalas. I don't think we could have survived without them.

For years, Meeru couldn't stop thinking about that stocked freezer: If Omi's frozen masalas tasted that good, couldn't we skip the step of adding protein or vegetables and create full-on curries, freeze them, then sell them? For people who want to eat well but don't have time to cook? Here was an opportunity to test the market and see whether there was an appetite for it.

Not every Indian restaurant needs to do takeout. I knew that crab, sablefish, and rare meats would be ruined by foil packaging, which blunts and muddies spicing. Still, I understood that sometimes you just don't feel like going out to eat. That was the impetus behind the special line of curries we created to launch with Rangoli. Our Vij's At Home line is essentially frozen takeout. That's the only way to retain the flavours of our curries.

From the start I felt that we could take the packaged meals across Canada. Not everyone could come to Vij's, but with the frozen line, Vij's could come to Regina, to Hamilton, to Moncton. We could take the business to the next level and make Vij's a national brand.

And restaurants have a shelf life: What's hot today might go cold in six months when the next big thing comes along. It's a tough industry. Many of Vancouver's most popular restaurants have had to shutter because food whims and fashions change so rapidly. Meeru and I are all too aware of the risks. If Vancouver cooled on Vij's, we were prepared with a new offering: Rangoli, Vij's hip younger sibling.

The name came from Mama. It's a reference to rangoli, the Indian art form in which beautiful patterns are created from rice, coloured sand, and flower petals in front of a house; the idea is to create something so spectacular that God will fall in love with the image and grant the home's owners prosperity.

We enlisted designer Marc Bricault, one of our regulars, to design the new space. We'd first met the Sault Ste. Marie, Ontario, native when he was a woodworker with a millwork shop on Granville Island. He'd come to Vij's, then on Broadway, on the urging of a pal. Eventually, he was coming so regularly that he became a close friend. He would go on to play a key role in the business, designing all our restaurants and pretty much everything inside them.

Marc is self-taught in all manner of design. Over the years, he evolved from creating furniture for architects to designing the interiors of apartments and small spaces. At the time, he built everything himself in his shop. Eventually his practice grew to a full-service design firm for personal and commercial projects throughout North America and Europe.

His first project for us, the whimsical elephant-pattern lanterns that decorated the Granville Street space, may be his most lasting. The die-cut lanterns cast dozens of incandescent dancing elephants along the restaurant's walls, an elegant, playful effect.

And these were no ordinary elephants. Marc knew of my roots in Bombay, the fast-paced capital of Maharashtra. The elephant-headed god Lord Ganesh is considered the western state's patron saint, and every fall, during the Ganesh Chaturthi, the festival celebrating his birth, his effigy is carried through the streets of Bombay to the Arabian Sea. These processions are far from sombre: The idols, some as high as fifteen feet, are accompanied by throngs of men and women dressed in a riot of magenta, saffron, and burgundy, singing and dancing their way to the seashore, a motley orchestra of ringing bells, thumping drums, and the reedy nadaswaram.

So instead of simply using an image of the god, Marc used that merry celebration as inspiration for the playful image he created: In it, the elephant's trunk and tail are pointed upward, signs of good luck, and the animal is dancing under the stars. The image stuck. The dancing elephant would go on to become our logo. It's on our menus, our labels, our cookbooks; it's painted, five feet high, on the brick wall outside Vij's. Meeru has had the Vij's elephant cast into a silver pendant, which she wears on a chain around her neck.

Over the years, I've stuck with Marc. He designed the interiors of Rangoli, My Shanti, and the new Vij's on Cambie Street. He came up with everything from the pillows and the ponds to the menu layouts, the take-home bags for the frozen line, and the tiny tin masala spice jars we sell at Rangoli. He even conceived the racks for them—made to look like highly abstracted elephants carrying the spices on their backs.

Marc feels that as soon as you open a restaurant's door, the room should signal that you're in for a very different experience. A restaurant's design is meant to mirror, even elevate, its driving ethos. Our spaces should reflect our take on modern Indian cuisine, which is in turn heavily influenced by our surroundings. That's even apparent in Marc's cheeky bathroom addition: At Rangoli, tiny TV screens run Bollywood song-and-dance routines on a loop, giving the bathrooms a retro, techie feel here in Vancouver's high-tech hub. (The concept was quickly copied by a major B.C.-based restaurant chain; imitation, I suppose, is the sincerest form of flattery.) At the time it was hard to source screens that small, so we bought them from a company that sold them to taxi cabs.

Nothing Marc does is easy. In the end, Rangoli ran a quarter of a million over budget. But he showed us the business value of investment in design. We were awarded Gold, for Best Design of the Year, by *Vancouver Magazine*. Ambience, we have always believed, draws guests.

Almost everything in our restaurants is made locally and by hand: our plates and bowls, lamps, tables, and even the bar, with its intricate mosaic tiles. It's a costly choice, and one I've occasionally had to fight to get past Oğuz, our CFO. At the end of the day, I'm deeply loyal. And Marc always does great work—whimsical, inventive, elegant.

At this point, his innate understanding of the company culture means he can design new spaces almost without speaking to us. If we mention that we need a picture to fill a space on the wall or pillows for a bench seat, he'll know without asking what Meeru and I might like. He's stubborn. He knows what he wants. And it's rarely the cheaper option. But he always comes armed with facts, and I trust his opinion.

Generally he'll bring Oğuz and me three options, and he'll hide the option he likes best in the middle: He knows we won't accept the cheapest option, or the priciest. In the end, what it comes down to is, we trust his taste. And we trust him.

At Rangoli, Marc removed everything inside except the walls and skylight. While Vij's is intimate and exotic, he wanted Rangoli to be fun and whimsical. He installed floor-to-ceiling windows, throwing in tons of light and allowing pedestrians a glimpse at the action inside. A skylight shaft painted bright pink casts a warm glow at midday, when the restaurant is busiest. The interior, including the floor and the tiled walls, is all done in red, meant to recall earthy Indian spices and the red-brown hues of our chai.

Marc maximized the tight room, using layered glass panels to carve out a tiny, tidy kitchen from the dining space with seating for thirty (an additional twenty-two can be seated on the all-season patio). Along one wall, a row of seven glass-fronted freezers are neatly packed with our line of fifteen frozen curries.

I once joked to a reviewer that our beautiful Herman Miller chairs were just uncomfortable enough that no one would linger. That, of course, wound up in his review. But as the concept evolved, we began wanting people to dawdle. Originally, it was meant to be an eat-and-go lunchtime spot, serving guests quickly and getting them out the door. Restaurants operate with a very different strategy for nighttime service, where diners can expect to remain at their table for hours at a time. Slowly, as we built our clientele and reputation, we pushed our close at Rangoli to eight p.m., then ten.

★

When we launched Rangoli in February 2004, we were trying to provide the craft and competence of the Vij's experience at the more modest charge of $10 a plate. Vij's is the restaurant for your wedding anniversary. Rangoli is your restaurant for blue jeans, its food cooked by the same hands but with a different ambience and price point. Whereas the more expensive tenderloin of beef goes to Vij's, the less expensive stewing beef goes to Rangoli.

The lunchtime menu at Rangoli was just four dishes: one fish, one curry based on a meat, like lamb, a vegetarian dish, and maybe something like a yogurt and tamarind–marinated grilled chicken. The point was to make something small, simple, and delicious. Since each curry came with rice, naan, and salad, you wouldn't lose time puzzling over a menu. You had only one choice to make: fish, meat, or veg.

Rangoli earned solid reviews and began racking up restaurant awards. The frozen line did phenomenally well from day one. But from a purely financial standpoint, the café side of Rangoli was not a success in its first year; Vij's was still so ingrained in everyone's mind that few seemed willing to give it a shot. It took two years and the efforts of our new manager, Oğuz Istif, before Rangoli was jam-packed. That was a huge challenge, and tough to manage.

At first, we could not seem to fill those seats in the evening, and nobody was coming in for lunch. It was as if a wedding was happening next door at Vij's every night. It's hard to leave the party, the excitement. We realized that Vij's was sucking the life out of Rangoli. We had to change that. I sometimes say that Vij's and Rangoli are like two daughters: It felt like my older daughter was hogging the spotlight, not allowing my younger daughter the opportunity to show her own individual beauty, to shine.

To drum up business, I would take the hands of people waiting to get into Vij's and guide them instead to Rangoli: "You'll enjoy it, I promise," I'd tell them. By then I'd become a draw. Sometimes people would walk by Rangoli and see me inside: "Vikram is there," they'd say. "Let's go in." For four months I didn't leave Rangoli. I didn't even check up on Vij's. It helped.

Sometimes, during lunch hour, I'd stand on the street and ask people walking by, "Have you had lunch yet? Come with me; try my new restaurant." You'd be surprised by how often the gambit worked. Then on Monday nights, I began offering cooking classes in Rangoli's kitchen. That helped, too.

Slowly, we built a customer base and a buzz. I remember being so excited the first day we sold $100 in wine. Rangoli was so casual that no one ever considered having a beer with lunch. Eventually, Rangoli started to capture a percentage of overflow from Vij's and a clientele of its own, often people who liked Vij's but not the wait. (Until the original Vij's closed in 2015, moving to our new, larger location on Cambie Street, Rangoli consistently drew 20 percent of its business from the lineup at Vij's.)

Although we'd worried that the lower price-point restaurant might eat into business at Vij's, those fears proved unfounded. That's the model. With all our restaurants, we tend to focus on volume in order to help bring down the cheque per person. High-end restaurants tend to serve fewer people but at a higher average cheque. The reverse is true of us: Our cheque average is lower, but we'll serve more customers. That's important to me. I want as many people as possible to be able to enjoy our food.

★

By 2005, when our manager at Rangoli had moved on, we initiated a search for a replacement. That's when Oğuz Istif, a Turkish-trained restaurant manager, first joined the team. Oğuz had arrived in Vancouver a few weeks earlier, and was looking for work. He'd come to B.C. with Kari, his Saskatchewan-born wife, after spending a single frigid winter in Saskatoon, her hometown. Oğuz hadn't much liked the prairie cold, or the tiny local restaurant industry where he was nicknamed "the Turk." If they were going to stay in Canada, they figured, they'd move to the warmest part of it.

Oğuz had met Kari while the two worked at an international school in Tarsus, near the Syrian border, in 1999—she as a teacher, he as a school administrator. He was educated in Turkey and had trained in its bustling hospitality industry, specializing in front-of-house operations.

On arriving in Vancouver, Kari quickly found teaching work. One day, shortly after they arrived, they happened to be sitting at a coffee shop across from Vij's. Oğuz was working on his CV when Mike Bernardo sat down at the table next to him and struck up a conversation.

When Mike mentioned that Rangoli was looking for a manager, Oğuz said, "That's what I do." Then, when Mike asked him to email his résumé, Oğuz said, "Let's make it formal. Give me your card, and I'll call you tomorrow to set up a meeting."

Meeru met him first, at the tail end of Mike's interview. She liked him from the second they shook hands. Oğuz is warm, polished, and inspires confidence. We hired him on the spot. Meeru describes him as the love of her life, though not romantically. She treats Oğuz like her little brother. And I treat Mike like mine. Mike and I are plugged into the city and the local restaurant scene, and we watch each other's back.

Oğuz reminds me of myself. He's independent. He's an

outsider. He knows what it's like to immigrate to a country where you can't speak the language, what it's like to go to the grocery store to buy milk and then get lost amid the twenty different varieties. We're fighters. We're survivors. And we're both macho Asian guys who love to wear pinks and purples and cologne.

Mike and Meeru tend to be more emotional. I tend to trust my gut when making decisions. But Oğuz is analytical, calm, and rational. And Oğuz, like me, is never satisfied. He's always challenging himself.

That's why he originally lasted only eighteen months managing Rangoli, where he was responsible for bringing up the café business and creating a regular and permanent clientele. A year and a half in, he'd done all he could to improve the place, and himself. As much as he loved Rangoli, and us, he'd plateaued. He didn't want to try managing a different restaurant; the problem would remain. He needed a new challenge. So he decided to go back to school to earn a Master of Business Administration at the University of Guelph, the only Canadian university offering an MBA specializing in hospitality.

He and his wife had toyed with staying in Toronto after Oğuz's 2007 graduation, but with a brand-new baby girl, they felt they needed to be in a place where they had a community. For Oğuz, Saskatoon was out. Kari felt the same way about Istanbul. So it was back to Vancouver.

As soon as Meeru and I heard the news, I offered Oğuz the newly created CFO position. We needed someone who knew numbers. We knew he'd be perfect in the role. It remains one of the best decisions I've ever made.

But I worried that Mike's feelings might be hurt, so I sat him down: "Your job is to manage operations," I explained. "Oğuz's job is to manage money. We need operations to tell the front-of-house what to do. And we need someone to closely track accounts. You can be the world's busiest restaurant, but not make any money." I needn't have worried. Mike and Oğuz have become close friends as well as colleagues.

We put Oğuz right to work: We needed to come up with an unassailable business plan for the Cambie project, our new signature restaurant, to present to RBC. When he returned in 2007, we'd just bought the land for it. By then it was clear that we'd outgrown our location on 11th Avenue. It would take another eight years to develop. But I'll have to come back to that story later.

★

A funny thing was happening with Rangoli. The frozen curries were selling so quickly that we couldn't keep the freezers stocked. The servers were spending too much time bagging frozen curry and too little time waiting tables. It was completely unexpected, the reverse of what we'd anticipated. We suspected we had a hit on our hands. But we knew it when Whole Foods, the first grocery store to offer them for sale, reported strong sales.

By then we were running two kitchens with separate stoves. One was used exclusively for making the bagged curries; it ran all day long, with a pot of whatever we planned to bag and sell that day. Beside the stove was a funnel used to fill the bags: We'd place a bag on the scale and then pour until we hit three hundred grams. Somehow, we also managed to squeeze in a blast freezer to flash-freeze them.

The original curries sold for $13 at Rangoli; theoretically, you could eat more cheaply at Rangoli than at home. To open up our market share, we knew we needed to drop the price point, but getting there with such small batch sizes was hard. We were a mom-and-pop operation, cooking our bagged curries during service lulls. And we refused to cut any corners when it came to quality.

We needed to ink bigger, better deals with suppliers and expand from our tiny storefront into grocery chains. Our first big deal was with Capers Community Markets (which was later purchased by Whole Foods). We're now in Choices Markets and IGA Marketplace and available nationally, through Loblaws.

Another early struggle involved finding the right packaging so that the takeout line could be reheated to taste as cleanly as when it's packaged. Meeru also wanted our waste footprint to be as small as possible. We settled on lightweight aluminum bags.

The silver bags Marc designed were made from the same technology NASA used to send food to space. The bright, shiny silver was also meant to recall tiffin boxes, used to carry lunch in India's business districts.

We had to track down a supplier willing to meet the relatively small number of bags while also keeping the price down. Eventually, we found one in Korea. Our specifications were relatively simple: We needed a multilayer material that could be heat-sealed in our kitchens. We didn't have room for a sealer or any other additional equipment.

Nor could we afford to buy individual printed bags for each product, so Marc came up with a cheaper alternative: stickers. The chefs would label the bags before pouring the hot curries into them. Eventually, we moved from silver to the black bags we use now (we'll soon begin transitioning to white bags).

Since manufacturing was new to us, we consulted with the British Columbia Institute of Technology (BCIT) on some of our health and safety questions: Are we packing the bags properly to prevent contamination? Where does bacteria grow? How do we avoid E. coli? BCIT also helped us develop tests to determine the shelf lives for all our products. We needed to figure out exactly which day our food would spoil, when our vegetables would begin losing their firmness, when our flavours would begin deteriorating.

At that point, Vij's at Home gourmet line took on a life of its own. The demand from local specialty stores expanded to larger grocery chains. And with more and more grocery stores starting to stock it, we bought a blue Prius to assist with deliveries. We soon realized, though, that we couldn't bring the meals' price point beneath $9.99 unless we began mass manufacturing them. Our kitchen operation at Rangoli just wasn't going cut it.

I was forty-five when we broke ground on our manufacturing facility.

VIJ'S INSPIRED INDIAN CUISINE

BY 2006, THE DEMAND FOR OUR packaged meals was outstripping the lunch rush at Rangoli. It was incredible. But growth of the frozen line was capped by what we were able to produce in the restaurant's tiny kitchen. That told us everything we needed to know about what our next venture should be. The time had come to build a manufacturing facility.

Some people read. I play chess. My grandfather taught me to play when I was a boy. The game is a perfect metaphor for life, or mine, anyway. I'm constantly at battle, always strategizing, plotting two moves ahead, quietly pushing a pawn forward when really I'm devising a plan for my king. Businesses chart their own futures through the long-term strategies they pursue. And in the high-stakes, fast-changing restaurant world, you can't stand still. To survive, you need a tactician at the helm, not just a CEO.

I didn't want to source out production because I wasn't willing to risk losing control of quality. For us, taste has always been the driver. We're not building a brand. We've built a reputation. When you eat Vij's food, you know the spices have been hand-roasted, the produce is farm fresh, that our meats were painstakingly sourced, that we've spent years perfecting the recipe. This means when you take a bite, it's guaranteed to taste delicious. The success of our frozen line would hinge on maintaining that signature.

"Just rent," Meeru urged when I first proposed the factory. But I wanted to buy the land. I wanted to build from the ground up. Meeru worried that I was taking on more debt than we, as a couple, could handle. She might have been right. A few months earlier we'd bought space on Vancouver's Cambie Street. By then, it was clear that Vij's had outgrown the 11th Avenue location. We planned to reopen our flagship on the busy West Side corridor.

There was another reason behind the factory. When I turned forty, I promised myself that by the time I was fifty I would have launched five major businesses: one for each decade of my life. They're not just restaurants; each is a marquee project. They are my children. Each is unique, beautiful.

I was forty-five when we broke ground on the factory. I knew that at forty-five I had the energy to take on this massive undertaking, just as I knew that five years from then I might not.

So in 2008, as the global economy collapsed and companies were downsizing or shuttering construction projects, we committed to building a production facility in Cloverdale, B.C., south of Surrey. From the start, we'd wanted our frozen curries to be a mainstream purchase, meant for everyone; with the factory at Cloverdale, a $6.5 million project, we worked hard to bring down their price point.

First, we had to come up with a business plan, part of our loan application to the Business Development Bank of Canada. Banks will lend only to businesses that are already performing. When you get a business loan from a traditional bank, your first interest payment is due within thirty days. You have to be that close to making a profit. An entrepreneur's growth projections mean little to them. They just want their capital back, plus interest. They have no stake in the company's growth. Their concern necessarily focuses on risk.

So we sought financing from the BDC. Its mandate is to help develop Canadian businesses through financing, growth, and transition capital. Interest rates are higher, but the loans come with more flexible repayment terms. Still, the BDC needed to see that I was willing to put skin in the game. I had to borrow money against our house in order to put up $800,000 of my own.

The loan process was insanely complicated and time-consuming; at one point, I was spending so much time at the BDC I joked that I should rent office space from them. Had the BDC come back and said "We can't fund this," I would have said "Fuck it" and backed out. But the BDC firmly believed in our vision and loaned us $3.8 million.

Meeru thought we should start small, at 5000 square feet. But I'd consulted with a number of local manufacturers, including Nature's Path, the Richmond, B.C.–based organic food makers. They all shared the same advice: Don't build small. You'll be fine for the first few years, but when demand surges, outpacing supply, you'll have to either expand or break ground on a new factory. The advice boiled down to this: Build it once, and build it big. For us, that meant much higher expenses and greater risk.

In 2008, the demand could have readily been met with a 3000- to 5000-square-foot facility. Instead, we built a state-of-the-art

28,000-square-foot factory that gave us plenty of room to grow. We were relying on predictive modelling to try to determine consumer and commercial demand. That's a fancy way of saying that we were guessing what demand might look like two, five, and ten years down the road. And sometimes we guessed wrong. (We've inked major deals with Safeway, Choices, Whole Foods, Save On, Thrifty's, and Loblaws. But it's meant that for the last five years we've been losing $50,000 a month, swallowing losses totalling $3 million—not pretty.)

Meeru hates debt, and the factory unleashed some ugly fights between us. By then, we'd almost finished paying off the mortgage for the house, and here I'd gone and borrowed more against it. Meeru doesn't have any security: If something happens to me, she and the girls will be in serious trouble. She'll be left to deal with it all.

The factory altered both our relationship and our lifestyle. Until 2009 we'd been relatively well off, pulling in $60,000 a month with Vij's and Rangoli. We paid each other $80,000 a year, never more. We could afford holidays, a comfortable life. By 2010, all this had changed. With the purchase of the Cambie Street building, the factory site, and construction costs, making monthly payments at home and work had become increasingly difficult. We weren't starving or uncomfortable, but we had to cut back on a lot. We all create lifestyles, and suddenly we could no longer maintain ours. Neither could we dismantle it and start fresh. We cut back on just about everything, including kids' activities, but not on our grocery bills. It was more important for us to feed them well. The stress I've brought into our lives was entirely my doing, and I hate what I've put my family through.

The margins in manufacturing are entirely different from those in the restaurant industry. Labour and food and overhead costs are structured differently. None of the principles we'd come to rely on in the restaurant industry applied—to steer clear of spaces where rent, for example, is more than 10 percent of sales. But then, tried-and-true rules are never the only consideration. You can't make every decision based on numbers. Just because something has profit potential doesn't mean it's a good idea. And vice versa: Just because it seems like a good idea doesn't mean it will make money.

I thought the factory would generate revenue within two years. It's been five, and only now is it inching toward the 20,000-bags-per-month break-even threshold. But this is all about the long game. To be successful in business, you can't get frightened off by initial losses, no matter how big.

At this point last year, we were at minus 37 percent. Right now, we're at only minus 11 on the year to date. We've got six months to go to close that gap, with several big accounts that will take us past the threshold. Vij's, the main restaurant, will always be our pillar, our flagship, but I believe the financial pole could one day shift to the grocery line of fifteen frozen meals, which include Mother-in-Law's Pork Curry and Coconut & Ginger Green Beans. The frozen curries have become a major strategic arm of the business.

★

We opened the factory in 2011, after three years of construction. Generally, I find that every new project takes twice the time and three times the cost of initial estimates. The two-storey building, which is painted bright orange, yellow, and green, stands out among the forest of grey factories that surround it. Upstairs we have a test kitchen and office space; on the first floor we cook, bag, freeze, and store the curries.

We chose Cloverdale, a small farming community that has since been swallowed by Surrey, for two reasons: comparatively cheap land and proximity to the U.S. border. The end goal was to go east, to break into Ontario, and then to move south. Right now, we're gunning for United States Department of Agriculture (USDA) approvals.

But getting Canadian Food Inspection Agency (CFIA) approvals has been an arduous, multi-year process, which helps explain some of the cost overruns: We thought certification would be more immediate—a period measured in months, not years. But once we've cleared that hurdle, USDA approvals will be relatively straightforward, and we'll have trucks within a five-minute drive of the U.S. border.

In October 2016, we finally received CFIA certification allowing us to sell our meats across Canada, not just in B.C. Only our vegetarian line is nationally available. And meats, we know, always outsell vegetable dishes. Consumers seem to value protein over vegetable dishes; they're more willing to spend $7.99 for the Punjabi Lamb Curry or Coconut Beef Curry than $6.99 for the Curried Chickpeas or Saag & Paneer.

But my biggest concern, beyond the regulatory headaches, was how to preserve the curries' unique and beautiful flavours through the large batching, processing, and packaging process. I wanted to make sure that when you cook the curries at home your kitchen fills with the intended aromas and that the flavours and spicing remain intact.

Though it seems self-evident, it's worth saying that making

one of something is quite easy. Consistently making lots of something is extremely hard. Scaling up was a brutal process. It's not as simple as just adding ten times the garam masala, onions, and coriander. It took a year of twice-daily test batching and sampling to perfect flavour profiles. To do it, Meeru moved eight cooks from Rangoli to the factory. They perfected the recipes there. We now keep a full-time staff of eight in Cloverdale, overseen by a former Rangoli manager.

Some of the failed experiments we gave to staff. Others were sent to Rangoli to be fixed or refashioned. Some became entirely new dishes and were sold at the restaurant. And some of it, I'm sad to say, ended up in the compost. We have rigorous standards. We'll never allow others to eat food we deem subpar.

We had some other major mishaps. At first, the bags would open when they hit the boiling water. So they had to be returned to the manufacturer, to be redesigned. And a $110,000 machine I had custom-built to scoop curry into the bags misfired: Rather than scooping a precise number of pieces of meat, the depositor would simply ladle the curry at random—sometimes three pieces would land in a bag, sometimes twelve. So we now do it by hand. The machine I still own—I can't bear to get rid of it. One day, I'll find some use for it.

And although it's a factory, we haven't fully automated the process. We never will. We try to infuse as much of the passion and love of food into the packaged product as possible. Most factories buy pre-chopped vegetables, minced garlic, mixed spices—it saves a lot of time and money. But there are significant flavour differences in a bag of chopped onions. So we buy our veggies whole, local, and fresh. The garlic, ginger, and onions are peeled and sautéed by hand. The cooks stir the curries themselves, as if they were warming on the stoves at Rangoli or Vij's.

And we continue to hand-sift, roast, and mill our spices every week at the factory. I firmly believe that that's the difference you'll taste in our home curries. When you walk into the production area you'll be hit with the smell of fresh ginger and aromatic spices. In the early morning, the cooks prepare and dice the meat by hand in a cold red room. The veggies are prepped in an adjacent room, painted green. The curries are then mixed in giant 300-kilogram stainless-steel steam kettles, enough to fill nine hundred 300-gram bags.

Once cooked, the curries are hand-packed in boil-in-bag pouches and then immediately plunged into an ice bath. So begins the high-speed freezing process meant to preserve the foods and keep them fresh; this brings the product from eighty, to four, then to minus thirty-two degrees over thirty-five minutes.

We refused to add preservatives, and found that even natural preservatives like lemon juice nullified the flavours. Pasteurization, a typical low-cost means to preserve food, was another option, but it turned the spicing bitter and dull. The tender, perfectly cooked meats grew rubbery. And everything came out tasting like chili. So we opted for blast freezing, a pricier, more elaborate option.

At home, the ready-made meals are cooked like pasta: You boil them in the bag in a pot for fifteen minutes or so while you crack open a bottle of wine and warm some naan. You can make the curries your own by adding fresh cilantro, yogurt, or chilies.

I love television—the stage, the excitement, the potential it opens up. I learned a lot in my season in the "Den."

Dragons' Den

I LOVE TV FOR THE SAME REASON I love being on the floor at five-thirty when Vij's opens for the night: I love people, the stage. I'm nothing if not a frustrated actor. And TV, of course, also helps solidify you as a serious chef. It has power, the ability to influence consumers. It gets your name out there. It helps create connections with potential customers who might remember the chubby chef when they're in the freezer aisle later that day. An approachable business owner will always make the product more approachable.

By 2011, I was doing more and more television appearances. From 2011 to 2013 I was a judge on *Top Chef Canada*, Food Network Canada's highest-rated program, which pits the country's top chefs against one another. In 2014, I judged the first season of *Chopped Canada*, which tasks chefs with creating original three-course meals. I was also judging *Recipe to Riches* alongside marketing guru and television personality Arlene Dickinson. On *Recipe to Riches*, home cooks from around the country compete to have their recipes become President's Choice products.

Arlene and I got along famously. She talked me up to Tracie Tighe, executive producer of CBC's *Dragons' Den*, who called me up out of the blue one day: "Come audition," she said.

At that point, *Dragons' Den* was the most watched entertainment property on CBC, with two million people across the country tuning in to every episode. The concept had originated in Japan in 2001, and was popularized by the British. Canada was one of roughly thirty countries around the world producing their own version. I was flattered, but at that point I'd been doing serious TV for only two years. I didn't feel ready. But Tracie kept hounding me.

I conceded eventually, but refused their request to don a suit and tie for the audition. I don't even own a jacket, let alone a suit. I've got nose rings and toe rings. I wasn't prepared to give up my soul, who I am, just because I was keen on the role. Instead, I went dressed the way I appear every night at Vij's: long sherwani jacket, tight fitted pants, no socks, Indian slippers, jewellery. That's who I am. I wanted to bring my own character to the show.

I went into the audition feeling totally confident and comfortable, and hit it out of the ballpark. The next day, I picked up Tracie downtown, at Vancouver's Sutton Place Hotel, and took her to my food truck on Georgia Street. She walked around the downtown core with me. I think she wanted to gauge my popularity firsthand. In Vancouver, people come up to shake hands and talk to me. It was the spring of 2013, and we popped into the winter farmers' market at Nat Bailey Stadium, across from Queen Elizabeth Park in Mount Pleasant. Same reception there. I'm approachable—in my restaurant, on the street, in coffee shops. I love talking to people. I adore meeting people. I have only one setting: I'm always on.

At the end of the day, Tracie said, "Everyone adored you."

Before I could become a Dragon, though, an existing one had to step down.

For months after that I heard nothing further, and figured they'd chosen someone else. Then one day Tracie and four top producers and CBC executives showed up at Vij's at the height of the dinner rush to deliver the news that I had been chosen for the show. Holy fuck, I thought. I was thrilled. But I didn't tell a soul. I'm deeply superstitious. When Meeru was pregnant with Nanaki I refused to talk about or even acknowledge the pregnancy. I never expressed any excitement until I was holding that perfect, healthy baby girl in my arms. Only then did I whisper a silent prayer. I'll never tempt the gods by speaking of something before it's set in stone.

The CBC first had to do a background check to make sure I was sufficiently legit—that means rich enough—to participate. We had to open up the books to them. As soon as the news broke, Shaw Media called. "We can't have you on *Chopped* anymore," my producer there told me. It was all network politics: If you're Rogers talent, you can't appear on Bell. I was now CBC talent. So I got chopped from *Chopped*.

I was so sorry to let it go. It's a great show, and I'd looked forward to mentoring young, up-and-coming chefs. It felt more in line with my core values, as a chef and as a person. But I knew that *Dragons' Den* represented the better business opportunity.

The first hint of trouble came when I donned my wardrobe for the first time: I looked terrible. My eggplant-purple shirt had turned a shiny brown under the harsh camera lights. For two days, I ran around Brampton hunting for a replacement with Lisa, a wardrobe assistant. In the end, we chose a dark achkan jacket over a creamy shirt with a Nehru collar.

I've always been self-assured, but the bright klieg lights, the cameras, the knowledge that I had to prove myself in a world that wasn't totally mine—I'm a restaurateur first, an entrepreneur second—made me uncharacteristically nervous. And I'm not ostentatious. I drive a Prius. I live in a simple home. Among the other Dragons, I was practically a peasant.

We filmed at CBC studios in downtown Toronto. The pitchers were penned into a hot tent outside. The nerves, the desperation, the tears make you realize the show's high stakes, and its cross-purposes: These folks were pitching their dreams. We were there to win the CBC ratings. A handful left the Den with new partners and funding. Some exited deeply embarrassed. But most, more than 75 percent, never even made it to air.

The show was a grind. Those long ten- and twelve-hour days under the lights take their toll. I stayed at Le Germain, in Toronto's Entertainment District, for the six-week shoot, living out of a suitcase. I'd come back every night and drink a bottle of wine by myself. I never went out. I wanted to remain focused. I'd wake early to meditate, to concentrate on the shoot ahead. Between takes I would study my notes. Things were hectic. At one point I was also filming the finale of *Recipe to Riches*.

Before the *Dragons' Den* filming began, I'd spoken with a local venture capitalist to get a sense of how to act on the show. "Be yourself," he advised. That's easier said than done. I quickly came to appreciate the old show business rule that says the toughest role to play on camera is yourself.

I spent days studying past episodes. And I think that all the preparation, the focus, backfired: I came in too prepared, too scripted, too tight. I needed to loosen up, relax a bit. I wanted to come across as smart and pragmatic, as someone who knew the system, who was prepared to walk away from a bad deal.

I'd thought I was hitting home runs. In reality, I'd struck out. My fairly minimal screen time was further cut by the editing process.

Between shoots, Arlene, Boston Pizza founder Jim Treliving, and *The Wealthy Barber* author David Chilton were always playing table tennis, to relax and kill time. They would badger me to join them, teasing me about how I had no game. Finally, I took the bait. In India, table tennis is serious business—and I schooled them with backspins and deep cuts. They'd had a magnum cup made, and I handily won their tournament. It was the only time I let my guard down.

During filming we were given no hint about who was up next or what they were pitching. The anger, the sweat, the frustration— that's all genuine. There's no script.

What's the secret to succeeding on the Den? The Dragons love big personalities, big ideas, big moxie. But you have to understand your market and your valuation. Screw that up, and they'll tear you to shreds.

I learned a lot about TV in my time in the Den. Ahead of taping it's essential to memorize a few one-liners and jokes you can pull out. Frustrated producers kept telling me that I needed to learn to explain myself in one sentence. That's a problem for me.

As a chef, I tend to be descriptive. Ask me to describe a cup of coffee, and I'll note that it's a dark, woody, chocolate colour near the rim, more reddish at the core, and brown where it's dried and oxidized. Producers don't want to hear any of this. They want you to say "The coffee is brown." "Get to the point," they kept barking into my earpiece. "Are you in or are you out?"

I found that if one of the other Dragons said something similar to me, my part was edited out. I used to ask a lot of questions, go back and forth with the entrepreneur. But the editing process cut everything except "I'm out." By the end, it looked as if you hadn't made any deals at all, Papa complained. "Most nights it seemed like there were four on one side with you on the other."

Arlene and Chilton knew to spend. They might not have gone ahead with the transactions in the end, but all the deal-making gave them plenty of screen time. I probably should have put aside half a million dollars just to ink deals on the show.

But I didn't want to risk coming across as careless for a few seconds of screen time. I wanted to be who I am: a restaurateur from India who has succeeded through hard work and smart choices. I'm not flashy. I'm not cruel. But that's what the camera loves.

They wanted another Kevin O'Leary, the Toronto business figure who'd left the show the season before. They wanted someone to vaporize contestants, label them "morons."

Sometimes it felt like the producers were throwing out bits of chum in order to stir the waters—to rile up the Dragons and give viewers a few laughs. That's not me. At times, it felt too mean. And I was too busy to abandon the restaurants for the six-week shoots. My Shanti had just opened in Surrey, and the new Vij's was about to launch on Cambie Street in Vancouver. So after just one season, we parted ways.

Oğuz was happy: My departure helped slow the flood of odd partnership offers he had to sift through—olive oil made with edible gold flakes was not even the strangest. And Meeru was thrilled: To her, reality TV represents everything that's wrong with the world. She despises it. She still hasn't seen a single episode of *Dragons' Den*. The more time I spent doing TV, the more strain I was adding to our marriage. Our growing debt load was also taking a toll.

It doesn't matter how good something seems; if you're not comfortable, you have to have the guts to say no. *Dragons' Den* is a great show, and it helps cultivate entrepreneurs, but the timing wasn't right for me.

Meeru and I have a very modern relationship. We've remained friends and formed a pact: Our new partners have to either be willing to join us at our family dinners or let us carry on as a family on Sundays with no hard feelings.

MY VERY MODERN RELATIONSHIP

FOR ME, THE FIRST SIGN OF INSTABILITY IN our marriage came a decade ago, with a massive fight over chickens, of all things. Those birds unsettled us. Meeru saw things differently. That we could fight so viciously over chicken signalled to her our shared commitment to fine food.

I'd wanted to start using Redbros, a French heritage breed, from Virginia Jacobsen's Polderside Farms in Yarrow, B.C. Local chefs consider Polderside's Redbros to be among the best poultry in the country. They're moist and flavourful, with a perfect texture. And the operation is humane; chickens are matured over ten weeks, roughly twice the pace of a commercial farm.

Instead Meeru wanted to use chickens from Thomas Reid Farms in Langley, B.C.'s first certified-organic chicken farm. They too produce an excellent bird, and for $1.50 less. To Meeru, it was a battle over a designer versus an organic chicken.

But I wanted us to be different. We were one of the first to buy the Redbros, which put us at the forefront of the local industry. A top chef wants to be always pioneering something new. I fought long and hard to bring them in, against the advice of Oğuz, Mike, and Meeru.

Although the Redbros were raised and culled locally, Meeru hated that the chicks were shipped from breeder stock in France. When the chicks arrived from Lyon, Jacobsen, who has since sold the farm, would have to drive in complete silence from the Vancouver Airport; otherwise, they would imprint on her voice and never let her leave the barn.

It was a stupid fight, looking back, but Meeru later told me she felt that I resented her role in the kitchen, that although we were partners, I wanted to make all the decisions. I thought she was being ridiculous: I felt strongly that the Redbros were a technically superior chicken, and I wanted the best for our customers.

By then, our business relationship was changing. From the outset, Meeru had always wanted to focus on the cooking. In the late 1990s she'd been content working in the background. At the time, she was new to Canada, new to motherhood, new to the restaurant industry, happy to be coming up with recipes, running the kitchen, and caring for her staff. Her contributions weren't being recognized and celebrated by media and the industry the way mine were, and she didn't give a damn: "No one knew I existed," she'll tell you. For the longest time, that never bothered her. Until it did.

She felt it made sense for her to do what she does best, and to allow me to handle the distraction of publicity on top of the role of CEO. The kitchen is her ballast. Even now, she'll tell you she's happiest at the end of the day, her fingers "stinking of onions and garlic."

But she isn't a professional chef, and in the eyes of local chefs, she didn't measure up because of it. If that stings, she'll never admit it. For a long time, none of that was important to her. The choice was also pragmatic. She was honing her skills, quietly con-tributing to the success of Vij's and Rangoli from the background. But for a long time, that meant her talent, her hard work, and the long hours she poured into our business were going unremarked. Everyone thought I was doing it all.

Over the years, a frustration and anger built in her: "Why do you take all the credit for being the chef of Vij's?" she exploded one day after I'd wrapped up a photo shoot. "It's not about the credit," I told her. "Do you want to do the cooking shows, the TV inter-views?" She hates that world. She thinks it makes chefs look like trained monkeys. I love it. That's where I thrive.

Then in 2006 we published our first cookbook, *Vij's: Elegant & Inspired Indian Cuisine*. With it, Meeru finally felt confident enough to get in the spotlight, with media attention, public talks, a stage of her own. The more she did, the more she liked it and the more she realized that she had an environmental and cooking message to share. And the more we butted heads.

She deserved all the accolades, the attention. But somehow, it threw our marriage off kilter. Where once we were working in unison toward a shared goal, suddenly there were two egos, unearthing new tensions, new rivalries.

That was also the point when she began referring to herself as Vij's "executive chef." It shouldn't have, but it made me angry. "Call yourself 'creative chef,'" I suggested. In the industry, among peers, we take the executive title very seriously: It denotes a high level of not just skill, but of training. Meeru was entirely self-taught. A nurse-practitioner in a rural area might deal with a lot of patients and effectively act as a doctor, but that doesn't make her an MD. She's a nurse, with tremendous chops and capacity. Meeru has never gone to chef school. She's never worked the line, or cut, or chopped, or been screamed at until she cried, or put in years of demeaning grunt work at a restaurant's lowest rung.

I'd gone to chef school in Europe. I'd done the training and put in the time. I'd started the business. Meeru plays an enormous role in the show, but I am its director. It's arrogance, I recognize it. We can be equals. But we can't sit on the same chair. We need chairs of our own. You can't take away a king's throne. A king will always fight for it.

At the same time, our shared vision for Vij's business future, and for our family's future, was splintering: Meeru was comfortable with our life. She just wanted to maintain. I badly wanted to take us to the next level.

"We're happily married," she'd say. "We love each other. We clear a half-million every year. We are the one percent. Why do you want to fuck with that?"

Meeru's tastes run simple compared with mine. She hates designer labels. Twice a year, she bargain-shops in New York's East Village with her sister, Ritu, who lives there. In Vancouver, she shops on Main Street, on the city's east side. For her, these extravagances are enough. "It's all landfill," she'll say. I, on the other hand, love the finer things in life. I love $1200 pants and Jo Malone cologne. I collect watches. Quiet and safe were never going to be enough for me.

It's not that she lacks drive. Meeru feels that in today's society no one is taught to be content, to be happy with what they have. We're taught to always want more. She's driven to maintain and be content at a level of income that's comfortable for her and her family. I didn't feel contented. It felt like we'd hit a plateau.

I left India to make something of myself. My life has been marked by hardship. Success has always been my goal—the point of the unending struggle. I'd arrived in Vancouver with nothing more than a few clothes and a strong work ethic. I knew I had so much more to give, and I wanted to build an empire, a legacy to leave our daughters. I wasn't content to stop and sit back.

For me, the factory was the point where I started to voice the vision I had for us. That was the first major rift. Meeru supported me, but she didn't like it. I was pushing pretty hard and she began pulling away. From the outside it was barely perceptible, but the relationship had begun to crumble.

Then in 2010, when we published our second cookbook, *Vij's at Home*, it was becoming obvious that after a decade and a half together, we were growing apart. I was on the Food Network. I judged on *Top Chef Canada* and *Chopped Canada*. My speaking gigs took me around the world. Developers were chasing me to open restaurants. I loved it. Meeru loathed it. She missed our "micro life," she kept saying. I couldn't wait for it to get bigger.

Every time I told her I wanted to create a legacy, to build an empire, she'd say, "I don't understand. I don't know why you'd want to do that." Our vision for the future was at odds. Meeru is extremely hard working, and she's brilliant. But at her core she doesn't have the ego I do. Over time, that became a big problem. She doesn't like to walk into a room and be recognized. I love it.

It all came to a head at a party in Tofino, in 2007. Sarah McLachlan was hosting a surprise fortieth for my best friend, Ashwin (they were still married at the time), at their woodsy, one-storey house on a stretch of pearl-white sand on Chesterman Beach. He'd had no idea. She and Ashwin had just had a baby girl, Taja, their second. Sarah had chartered a plane for their eight guests, mostly friends of theirs from work and neighbours from

West Vancouver; she was putting us up at the Wickaninnish Inn, at the beach's north end.

A decade earlier, Meeru would have jumped at the opportunity to take a private jet for a weekend without the kids. But in the past ten years she had become increasingly environmentally conscious. She'd begun grinding roasted crickets into flour to add protein to paratha flatbread in the name of food sustainability. She was a year away from introducing whole crickets at Rangoli. She put her foot down, and refused the offer of a flight: "We're putting the Prius on the ferry," she said. "How can I get out there and talk about climate change and the need to reduce our carbon footprint, then hop on a charter?"

"But the plane is leaving anyway," I replied. If it were the two of us chartering an empty plane I could understand, but even if we didn't get on the plane it would still leave the runway.

Meeru ended up calling a climate researcher at the David Suzuki Foundation. Ethically, she felt that people have to start making a point by altering their choices. This was her line in the sand.

To me, it felt like a whole lot of bullshit. I'm willing to take a stand on moral grounds. I do it all the time. But in this case, I couldn't understand how we were serving the planet by driving to Tofino when our two seats on the plane would remain empty. And we'd burn power—and take up a spot on the ferry—getting there. I was livid: It was my best friend's fortieth birthday.

Looking back, it was an intensely stupid fight. But it was a strange weekend all around. Sarah and Ashwin's marriage was falling apart. All the other couples, meanwhile, fit together like pieces of a puzzle, exposing, like a funhouse mirror, the ugly truth about our own marriage. The fight between Meeru and me had revealed, in excruciating detail, just how much we'd changed, how far we'd grown apart, how differently we saw the world and our place in it.

In the end, we took the ferry, arriving eight hours late to Sarah and Ashwin's. We had a fine time on the drive out, but all weekend, I couldn't chase the thought from my mind: Why couldn't Meeru play along, make one tiny exception for my happiness? And I know Meeru kept thinking, How can he put a party ahead of my feelings?

In hindsight, I think that was the beginning of the end for Meeru and me. We could no longer hide from the fact that we wanted different things, different lives. While I remained deeply committed to social justice, Meeru was growing singularly focused on saving the planet. It seems ridiculous, but we turned this into a marital issue. Meeru and I would last another three years, none of them good.

Our final fight, the one that broke the camel's back, was over My Shanti, my latest restaurant venture in Surrey. Meeru wasn't the only one skeptical of My Shanti. So was Oğuz. So was Mike.

In 2010, developers behind The Shops at Morgan Crossing, a proposed development for South Surrey, approached me with a business proposal. They had three restaurant openings in the open-air, California-style mall at 15765 Croydon Drive, a five-minute drive from the U.S. border. One went to Famoso, a western Canadian franchise that serves Neapolitan pizzas. The other went to White Spot, B.C.'s beloved burger chain. The developer, Wales McLelland Construction, wanted to offer us the third spot. New developments will often attempt to draw a big-name restaurateur to act as an anchor or a draw.

Oğuz didn't think suburbanites were our crowd. Whereas in Vancouver it might be common for a person to eat out once per week, Oğuz felt that those living in Vancouver's suburbs tend to invest a lot of money in large homes and, with young families, tend not to go out much. There's a reason why chain restaurants flourish in the suburbs, he used to lecture me; people prefer inexpensive family restaurants. I was unmoved.

I believed then, and still do now, that the suburbs are changing. They used to be for people who wanted out of the city, who wanted the big house. But things are different. No one can afford Vancouver anymore—not to buy, often not even to rent. Lawyers, engineers, journalists, dual-professional families are leaving—for Surrey, for the Tri-Cities, for White Rock. Even I don't own a home here anymore. I rent. And all these people still want to eat. Out there, it's a sea of Milestones, Kegs, Cactus Clubs. I thought we could give them another option, something entirely different. I also believed that the large nearby Indian community in South Surrey would help support us. Meeru was furious that I was willing to put us in even further debt for My Shanti when we were still in debt with the factory. She could not psychologically handle the debt load.

Mike also worried about the space we'd purchased on Cambie Street. By then the Cambie location had been sitting vacant for eighteen months, and our neighbours had begun writing to complain. It was an eyesore, some said. Mike thought we'd risk further angering our already frustrated neighbours if they got wind of a new project in South Surrey while the Cambie spot was left vacant.

In the end, it came down to a vote: the final count was 3 to 1, with only me voting in favour of the Morgan Crossing location. But I'm a stubborn person. When I think something is right, I shut my eyes to the naysayers and push ahead.

I know Meeru thinks it was my ego, my pride, that drove a stake between us. But there was something else at play: I wanted to create my own food. I felt cornered, restrained, like a musician forced to keep playing someone else's songs. As my business role had expanded over the years, the kitchens at Rangoli and Vij's had come to be Meeru's alone.

I needed to start playing a more creative role. That I was the CEO should have been enough, but it wasn't. I love cooking. I love creating. I felt stifled in the boardroom. I needed to create a kitchen of my own. So I went ahead with My Shanti against her advice; she was furious, and wanted no part of the project. That was her line in the sand. Oğuz oversees it, as he does all our business entities.

That fight further eroded our marriage, but for a while we tried to make it work. Ashwin, who was dealing with the collapse of his own marriage, was a constant support. We'd push each other to be true to ourselves. It's all so hard to figure out.

I made the decision to separate from Meeru when I was in India, in 2011. I went off alone, for a week, by myself. I travelled to Jaipur from Delhi and stayed five days. Mostly, I walked. I thought and I walked. When I needed it, I caught a few minutes' shut-eye—in parks, on sidewalks. I felt like a born-again Indian.

I ate street food at stalls on crowded boulevards. I slept on the trains. I didn't shower. My hair was a mess. I wore the same clothes. I was effectively homeless, and looked the part. I was tormented by my collapsing marriage. I needed to clear my head. I needed to think. Solitude does nothing for me. I don't want a cabin in the woods. I wanted to be on a sidewalk so crowded that you can't lift an elbow without touching someone. I craved the noise, the heat, the smells, the vibrancy, the colour of my India.

Over and over, I kept thinking, Can I live without Meeru? Can I do this to our family? Is this the right thing to do?

It's not, I would think, suddenly arguing with myself. So what if we fight? This is crazy: I love her so much. Papa and Mama are so different, but they stuck it out—they made it work. We can, too.

The next day, my resolve would return: I can't go on like this—the constant bickering, the ugly fights. I'm sure I looked insane, muttering to myself, my ripped cotton pants crusted with mud. Then again, it's India. It's so busy, nobody fucking cares.

Back in Delhi, I had a reservation at a decent five-star hotel. I took a yellow-and-green tuk-tuk from the train station, where I'd picked up my belongings. But security refused to allow the tuk-tuk on hotel grounds. They mocked me when I tried to tell them I had a reservation inside. "Go, go, go," a young security guard said, brushing me off. The driver stopped down the road, and I walked back. This time, security called the manager, who was shocked when he realized who I was and learned how I'd spent the previous week.

"Come, come, come," he said, ushering me straight up to my room without even checking me in. His office manager came up later to check me in himself. They must have been afraid of having a man looking so dishevelled walk through their lobby. I can't say I blame them. Shedding the week's accumulated grime took thirty minutes in a piping hot shower. But I'd come to a decision.

I felt that Meeru and I needed a break, a trial separation. We couldn't keep tearing each other apart. We needed some time to breathe. In my heart of hearts I knew we were done. I wanted to push the business further, and to do so, I knew we could no longer live under the same roof. It was that simple. I needed to set us both free.

I planned to tell her on my return from Delhi. I'm not an emotional guy. I'm a strategist. I don't move on impulse. Everything

I do, every step I take, is planned first. But working up the courage to tell Meeru what I'd decided was excruciating. The night before I told her I was a mess. I was tormented by the task ahead.

I couldn't sleep, so I got up and walked. Outside, it was raining. But I didn't care. I headed down to the seawall and walked and walked and walked. The city lights were dancing on the black waters along False Creek. I felt such sadness, such a weight on me. I was so alone, so ashamed. How would Nanaki and Shanik react? I wondered. How would this impact our business? Meeru and I had spent seventeen years building this brand as a couple.

Mostly, though, I wondered how Meeru would react, and how she would ultimately fare. She knew as well as I did what a mess our marriage had become, but I was the one initiating the separation. I would move out, and leave Meeru in our family home with the girls.

That night, I walked all the way to Jericho Beach, about ten kilometres from our home. When I finally made it back, dawn was starting to break. I had a smoke, alone in the yard. Then, finally, I was able to sleep.

"We need some breathing space," I told Meeru the next evening. "All we're doing is fighting." It had worn me out: I was exhausted, totally spent from month after month at war. I wanted us to try living apart for six months; I hoped a break might be all we needed. While she and I have always been great at talking and communicating, some things were difficult for me to express. I was fearful of hurting her, and meant to articulate that I wanted a trial separation. But when I saw a look of horror spread across her face, in a panicked attempt to fix it, I blurted out, "Don't worry, you're a lovely person, you will meet another man who will love you dearly." Instead of making her feel better, I'd insulted her further.

"If you walk out our door, that's it. I'm not going to let you walk back into my life as my husband—ever. I'll move on." And she did.

I loved her—madly, deeply. I still do. But she was driving me bananas. And I wanted the freedom to helm a kitchen, to be creative again, to be in charge of my own decision making. I'd gone to hell and back in Austria, in Banff, in Vancouver, working my way up in the industry. And in some way, though I've never been able to express this to her, I felt I was setting her free. She was miserable. She was being pulled in one direction and I was going off in another. It was unworkable. And it could never be resolved. We were being pulled to separate poles. Neither of us was at fault, not really.

I don't mean this in a shallow way, but I wanted to be known, wealthy, successful. She wanted something entirely different: a comfortable existence, a man with whom she can share long, deep conversations.

We were miserable, and I could see we would only continue to be. I thought I was freeing her to be happy again. I told her I planned to move out on January 1.

Nanaki and Shanik were devastated, but not exactly shocked by the news. We weren't able to hide our fighting from them. Both cried when we told them of our plans to separate. "We're kids with split-up parents now," Shanik remembers thinking. She had always divided her classmates into two camps: those with divorced parents and those whose parents remained together. She despised the move into the former camp. For a time, it caused her to act out.

When we fought, the girls used to take off together: They'd ride the SkyTrain downtown to skate at Robson Square and play on the iPads in the Apple Store at Pacific Centre. Afterward, they'd share a Blizzard at Dairy Queen. This became their ritual. It bonded them.

Growing up, they hadn't been close. Through this, they began sharing their feelings, how the turmoil at home was upsetting them. They learned to laugh it off. They became the best friends they are today.

My parents first noticed something was amiss at a dinner in October 2011, where I was awarded the Ernst and Young Entrepreneur of the Year Award. In my acceptance speech I didn't acknowledge Meeru. We were still living together; she'd even joined me that night as my partner.

"Why did he not mention Meeru?" I heard my dad ask my mom.

"Something is wrong," my mom concurred.

"They're following Ashwin and Sarah," my dad said. He knew that my best friend had split with his wife. "Vikram is following in Ashwin's footsteps." What a joke. As though I'd make such a grave decision simply because my friend was doing it.

A few weeks later, before I'd even told my parents, Meeru phoned my mom and asked her to intervene, to help halt the separation. Meeru was sitting in her car. It was winter, and she needed to speak privately, away from the girls.

"Tell him not to leave," Meeru begged my mom. "Tell him he's got a beautiful family, that he's making a mistake, that he needs to stay."

"Meeru, my dear," she said. "This is between you and your husband. You need to figure it out. I can't get between you." In the end, they spoke for so long the car's battery died and Meeru had to bring in a mechanic to jump-start it.

Mama was gentle, but firm. She wanted, with all her heart, for us to remain together, but she knew she could not intervene. And she trusted my decision. I was deeply moved by her response.

Later, I sat my parents down and explained that I was planning to move out. Right away my father's practical side chimed in: "You put the restaurant in her name!" he almost shouted. He wanted me to speak to a lawyer immediately. He worried that Meeru might try to sell it out from under us. The idea was ludicrous. Meeru is my business partner, and the mother of my daughters. I wasn't planning to change a thing about our business or our personal finances.

We've fought like thieves, but there is such beauty and good-ness in Meeru. Most people would have sued me for a 50/50 split and then walked away. She's never been mean or stingy about money. She's never taken a penny she wasn't owed from the busi-ness. If anything, she's made more sacrifices than I. Even through her anger, she has supported me when I wanted to take risks, to push us beyond where she was comfortable. She backed me, and trusted my judgment. Years later, we still share a single account. Whenever I give a paid speech or television gig, I put the money earned in that shared account. We're like two great friends living separately. In some ways, I think we'll always be one.

Our last night together was desperately sad. The four of us, Meeru, the girls, and me, went to see *My Week with Marilyn* at Tinseltown, a movie theatre in Vancouver's Chinatown neighbour-hood. When we got home, I cooked a pork roast. After dinner we walked to Kino Café, an intimate Spanish tapas bar on Cambie, to watch flamenco. We love the dresses, the guitars, the dramatic movements, the blur of reds and blacks. But it all felt so weird, so sad, so surreal: We all knew what the next day held, what lay ahead. But each of us wanted one last night together as a family. Each of us was choking back our tears. Each of us was pretending nothing was wrong when it felt like everything was.

I left home on New Year's Day, 2012. All of 2011 had sucked: We were drowning in debt—from the factory, from the empty space on Cambie. There was no light at the end of the financial tunnel. Meeru and I had been constantly fighting—at home, at the restaurant. There was so much raw emotion, shouted "Fuck yous!" The girls were furious with me for leaving. They blamed me. But even Meeru could see that we had run our course as a married couple.

The separation caused Meeru to rethink what she was even doing in Vancouver. At heart she's an East Coast, big city person. She loves a concrete jungle. She came to the West Coast for me. She'd left her home, her family, and her friends in Washington, D.C. And Meeru feels that ultimately I chose My Shanti over her, that she was dumped for a business opportunity. She'll tell you that she wishes another woman had been involved, that she would have preferred that. That it would have hurt less.

On the first day of our separation, I boarded a flight for Toronto. When I came home, I moved into a one-bedroom condo in the Olympic Village at the southeast corner of False Creek, a five-minute drive from home. It was the darkest point of my life.

For the longest time we'd had the perfect marriage. And I don't think either of us could have achieved such success on our own. But that same cataclysmic energy was also our undoing. Our love had grown volatile, spiteful. It was poisoning us.

I believe that once she finished struggling through the first year of our separation, Meeru grew happier and happier. She's dating someone now. I miss our life. I miss her. I still don't know whether the breakup was a mistake. There are times when I think, Should I have toughed it out? But we're both so strong-willed.

For the first year we lived apart, we did not make our separation public. Meeru wanted the privacy to grieve. She needed space to care for the girls, to make sense of it all for herself. We had to figure out how to move forward while creating as little collateral damage as possible. We weren't willing to lose our love, our business relationship, our friendship. But most importantly, we wanted to be loving co-parents, to figure out how to continue raising the girls together. And I didn't want us to become fodder for gossip in Vancouver, in the restaurant world. I didn't want us to lose focus on ourselves and suddenly spend time worrying about what others were saying. This was too personal. This was the worst pain of my life.

I can be guarded with the media. Meeru tends to be more of an open book. We agreed that unless people could know the full story—of our marriage, and how it fell apart—they did not need to know. Until we could explain it, we would not share it. So here, for the first time, is the story of how we lost our marriage but were able to rescue our love, our friendship, our business, our civility.

★

In the end, we weren't willing to give up our careers for our marriage. So we gave up our marriage for our careers. Our business partnership is stronger than ever. Meeru is even more involved in the business now. And although the marriage might have dissolved, the family remains strong.

Emotionally, I have never left Meeru. I will always be there for her. Almost every Sunday night we get together with the girls for dinner. For us, it's the most sacred thing we do. We've been very clear: No matter who we end up with, they have to be able to sit at the table with us on Sunday nights.

I visit my parents from four to six p.m., then arrive at Meeru's for six-thirty. We'll have a coffee and catch up. Then Meeru will go for a run, and I'll hang out alone with the girls. When she gets back, we all move into the kitchen together while I prep dinner—always vegetarian, for Meeru. She'll crack open a bottle of wine, make some guacamole, and cut up some veggies to snack on; then she'll make a salad. The music is always Meeru's or the girls' choice. None of them can stand my Bollywood music.

We'll have a nice, leisurely dinner. By then, we're onto our second bottle of wine. Just before ten, I'll head home for the night. It works. This is the happiest we've been in years.

It's a modern relationship, I suppose. We've remained friends, and formed a pact: Our new partners have to either be willing to join us at our family dinners or let us carry on as a family on Sundays with no hard feelings. If they aren't willing, they can't qualify for partner. We still give talks together. We do presentations together. We do interviews together. Late at night we'll still share a stolen cigarette. Until the day I die, I'll be aware of the pain I caused. That will forever haunt me.

Accepting the failure of my marriage was hard. I take some comfort knowing that Gandhiji's relationship with his wife was practically non-existent. That Nelson Mandela and Martin Luther King, men I admire deeply, lived totally screwed-up home lives. No human can be successful in every facet of their lives. They can't be the best lover, the best husband, the best father, the best coach, the best businessman. Something will always give. We're more like amoebas: We're never perfect. We're always a little crooked, a little misshapen, a little bent in one area, perfectly smooth and rounded in another. And for me, relationships are secondary to career. Success is my driving motivation, crass though it sounds. Going forward, my focus narrowed: to my restaurants and to my girls.

My Shanti is a reflection of the personal and culinary journeys that I've taken with friends throughout India. My explorations took me from the kitchens of home cooks and executive chefs to the ubiquitous street food stalls, exchanging ideas and discovering spice mixtures, ingredients and techniques.

My Shanti by Vikram Vij

MY SHANTI IS MY GEM. The new restaurant quite literally sparkles on the edge of South Surrey. Marc created this effect by giving its exterior a 50s Bollywood feel, covering the building in fifty thousand shimmering, silver discs to give the illusion of a giant, sparkling sari.

The sequins are lifted by the wind like ripples on a lake. But the effect is even more entrancing after sunset, when they twinkle, reflecting hot pink lighting. It wasn't easy to convince the City of Surrey to agree to allow us to do it. But that was nothing compared to the installer's job: It took him five months to hang each sequin onto J hooks by hand.

If My Shanti, "my peace" in Hindi, adopts an unconventional definition of tranquility, it's because I do, too. I find peace in noise, in chaos, in vibrancy, in colour, in India. My Shanti is an homage to the diversity and richness of the culture and cuisine I've experienced in my Indian travels—ten years of culinary pilgrimages that took me from the kitchens of home cooks to those of executive chefs and to the ubiquitous street food stalls, where I discovered new ideas, spicing mixtures, ingredients, and techniques. Some of my deepest friendships were formed along the way.

The flavours are as bold and deep and eclectic as the space. Inside, we adorned the walls with an immense, hand-painted Madhubani tapestry, the vivid, geometric mural-painting style practised in India's northern Bihar province. The form was relatively unknown to the outside world until the massive 1934 Nepal-Bihar earthquake, which left nineteen thousand dead; officials inspecting the damage were stunned by the art the quake uncovered, noting similarities to modern greats like Pablo Picasso and Joan Miró.

Increasingly, Madhubani artists depict social and political issues. At My Shanti, our tapestry shows a village scene, with animals living in harmony with villagers. We wanted to emphasize the importance of living in harmony here in B.C., where wealth and food are so abundant.

Getting the mural to Canada was no small feat. Marc tried reaching out to a Madhubani school in northern India, but he never heard back. After several months, he gave up and started sourcing alternatives to fill the wall space. Then out of the blue one day, he took a call from an anthropologist at U.C. Berkeley. For years the academic had been supporting Madhubani artists, and he ultimately helped us cobble together a deal for the massive work, the largest ever sold outside of India. I would speak in Hindi to the artist, Kamlesho Roy, late at night, so that he could explain the drawing and update me on its progress. But in the end, we had no real idea what it would look like. And when it finally arrived, in a five-foot FedEx box, I panicked: How could it be so small? Had I pissed away hundreds of thousands of dollars?

Then we gently pulled the fabric from the box. It was like origami. It had been folded thousands of times in tiny, interlocking squares, so intricately that its packing was practically art in itself. To hang the enormous artwork we had to hire six workers, who pulled it taut from every angle. The result is magnificent.

Lanterns made from bright, clashing saris hang from the ceiling. The golds and pinks—signifying hope and celebration—are meant to give the feel of an Indian wedding. By the patio, a bar modelled after a chai stand gives a village feel. The wall behind it is covered in vintage prints of Indian matchboxes, another great graphic tradition from the subcontinent.

With Indian food, people seem to think, It's fast, it's ethnic— it should be cheap. Sure, you can find a $10 curry. But the reality is that when you come to My Shanti, you're doing more than filling your belly. The menu took me ten years to build. You're experiencing a bit of the culture. And presentation, I have always believed, matters.

The menu might have taken years to develop, but it took just fourteen hours to write. Bright and early one Saturday, during the filming of *Dragons' Den*, I walked to Bar Buca in downtown Toronto, carrying my MacBook, intending to jot down a few thoughts. I sat there through breakfast. Then lunch. Then dinner. Then through two bottles of wine. I left at one a.m. with an entire menu, from the gol gappa—a shot of spiced lentils and potatoes with mint and tamarind that I'd had at a street stand in Lucknow, in Uttar Pradesh—to the slow-roasted duck biryani that had wowed me in Kerala.

The spice quotient at My Shanti is much higher than at Vij's, where the cuisine is more rooted in the French technique. Many dishes, like the wild boar kebabs, come with fruit chutneys to leaven the heat. My Shanti is a little more Indian: a little richer, a little spicier, a bit more playful, a lot more whimsical. For the first time in two decades I had the freedom to develop my own menu, all on my own. I had such fun.

I visualized every dish: What was that flavour that knocked the hell out of me at a street stall in Goa? How could I replicate that dry, dry goat with whole chilies I'd had on a searing afternoon in Bangalore? I'd kept detailed notes on my phone. But mostly, I worked from memory.

It's a creative process, and what you envision might come out entirely different, especially when trying to source ingredients locally. What starts as veggie samosas might become battered chickpeas. And that's okay. I felt like a composer creating an aria.

But not all of my experiments worked. A roasted chicken, served on the bone, was one memorable flop. I'd envisioned a table of people sharing it, tearing off strips and dipping them in the accompanying sweet sauce. My staff warned me that our custom-ers wouldn't know what to do with it. They were right: The dish failed miserably. People kept trying to awkwardly cut the meat from it using knives and forks. I'd encourage them to use their hands. But no one wanted to touch the bird, and tons of chicken was being returned to the kitchen. I couldn't stomach the waste. I quickly pulled it from the menu. My eyes have been opened many times by My Shanti.

At one point, in fact, I almost shut down construction: Cost overruns at the plant and building expenditures for Vij's Cambie Street location meant that I couldn't pull together the money we needed for My Shanti. But I wasn't willing to call it quits. So I assembled a group of four silent partners—four friends, including

Ashwin—who each put up an equal share in My Shanti and will receive a percentage of its earnings.

Construction was projected to run $1 million, but swelled to $2.2 million. Three years later, I still owe $1.2 million to Doug Scott, president of Wells McLelland Construction, the developer behind it. Doug's been calling and emailing, but the business just isn't there yet to repay that debt. I've had to sit down with him and look him in the eye and tell him that I don't have the money I promised him, a humbling experience, particularly since Doug is also a friend. His wife is a foodie, and they've come on all my trips to India, to Cambodia and Vietnam. I can tell he knows exactly how much it bothers me. That's my saving grace.

I still believe this is a great location. I've always believed in it. The neighbourhood's five-year growth projections look excellent. We just have to be patient. Closing My Shanti is not the solution: I'm on the hook for $1.2 million.

In My Shanti's first six months, the honeymoon stage, I felt like a genius: People flocked to us. Reviews were astonishingly good. *The Globe and Mail*'s restaurant critic, Alexandra Gill, gave My Shanti 3.5 stars, labelling the food "extraordinary." Mia Stainsby, of *The Vancouver Sun*, called the results "close to a nirvana experience." In the two years since it opened on June 2, 2014, My Shanti has been named B.C.'s "Best Indian" restaurant by *Vancouver Magazine*, knocking Vij's out of contention.

We were busy as hell at first, clearing $10,000 a night, even on weeknights. Within a year, we'd broken even—and in this industry it generally takes at least two. Sometimes Meeru would stop by for a drink on her way to Shanik in Seattle, which she'd opened in partnership with Oğuz. I could tell that it stung—seeing me sweat through the service, the dining room full, loud with laughter. She was hurting. Shanik was in a tailspin. The business, she and Oğuz had come to realize, was not viable. Then came my humbling—fast and hard.

Business declined over the 2014 Christmas season, then levelled off. Some nights we barely clear $3000. This ebbing was not unexpected: The same thing happened at Rangoli after the initial excitement wore off. But even on our worst nights we're still breaking even.

All our businesses have gone through it: In the beginning, Vij's supported Rangoli until we could get it up and running on its own. And for years, the three restaurants were supporting the factory, keeping it alive. Now the factory is finally solvent, but the restaurants are supporting My Shanti, their newest sibling. Still, it's an intensely stressful time.

But I keep working at the business, pushing to turn it around, re-evaluating the concept, tinkering with the menu, trying to drive My Shanti to the next level by sheer force of will. I know we just need to find one dish—a My Shanti equivalent of Vij's lamb Popsicles—to cement its reputation as a Surrey destination and to keep patrons coming back again and again.

I've learned a major lesson in Surrey: I am not borrowing another cent. I'm done sticking my neck out.

★

Last spring, amid the financial worries, I was awarded "Chef of the Year" at the Vancouver Magazine Restaurant Awards. The prize, a stunning achievement, should have gone to both Meeru and me. That was bad enough. But then I went up and made it so much worse: In my acceptance speech, I forgot to acknowledge Meeru, the most important person to me, both in business and in life, the person who had made all of it possible. You have moments of genius. Then there are the fumbles, perhaps to remind you just how human, how flawed, how shit you really are. It was a complete failure, and in front of all our co-workers and peers. It was unintentional, but it hurt her so much.

Here's what happened. The restaurant awards are treated like state secrets. Nothing is revealed in advance. Winners are given no hint they've placed. That night, we scored an unprecedented hat trick in the "Best Indian" category, picking up gold for Vij's, silver for My Shanti, and bronze for Rangoli. (The icing on the cake came when we learned that Vij's Railway Express had won silver in the food truck category.)

We'd cleared the podium. I was in shock. Minutes later, hearing my name called for "Chef of the Year," the night's biggest prize, blew my mind.

I had no speech prepared. I was in a fog. I managed to thank the event organizers, but I have no idea what I said. Somehow, I forgot Meeru.

She wasn't there that night. But a close friend was. She was told immediately of my gaffe.

Meeru was furious. Seeing her, I felt about an inch tall. I kept telling her how sorry I was. It was a genuine mistake. People forget what it's like to walk on stage, to face bright lights and a big crowd. The only good that came of it was that Meeru shared with me her hurt feelings, and I acknowledged her pain. But God, I still feel like such an ass. I'll never forgive myself for it.

Meeru and Oğuz join forces to open Shanik in Seattle.

SHANIK

SEATTLE FOODIES WERE ABUZZ, on May 10, 2012, at the news that Vij's was opening a sister restaurant in South Lake Union, a neighbourhood in the city's north. "OMG! OMG!" wrote a commenter on an article announcing the move in *The Stranger*, the Misty City's alt weekly. "The best restaurant in the universe is coming to Seattle!"

The proposal for the Shanik venture had come from Vulcan, the real estate development business launched by Microsoft co-founder Paul Allen. With My Shanti, my hands were more than full. I had no involvement in Shanik. This would be Meeru's and Oğuz's alone.

Over the preceding decade, Vulcan had been leading a fifty-five-acre neighbourhood redevelopment project in South Lake Union, once a low-rise, low-rent warehouse and shipyard district. There, Vulcan had erected a cluster of mixed-use office buildings and apartments. (Sometime after Meeru and Oğuz signed the agreement, Vulcan sold much of the development to Amazon, its main tenant.)

The setting was no accident. Rather than stick its workers in the suburbs, Amazon was choosing to position itself at the heart of humming, busy, crowded Seattle, using the appeal of bike paths, good restaurants, and museums as recruiting tools. Wooing tech talent is no easy game. Vulcan wanted a Vij's to help anchor the new development and become a nighttime draw.

Meeru and Oğuz scouted the street-level location and liked what they saw: Amazon had just moved in, flooding the streets at lunchtime with their workers (obvious in their blue employee badges). They number some fifteen thousand in Seattle, mostly engineers, managers, and programmers. Their average salary was in the mid $90,000 range. While it didn't much feel like a neighbourhood yet to Meeru, this didn't worry her. It reminded her of the breakneck regeneration of Yaletown, Vancouver's bustling former industrial neighbourhood, which has a heady nighttime scene.

"Do it," I told her when she returned. Our daughters, then in their teens, told their mom to practise what she preached and go for it. They weren't as much interested in another restaurant as they were in seeing their mom be a strong woman, push herself, and do something of her own. She named it Shanik in honour of our younger daughter. (Nanaki, our older daughter's name, is sacred to Sikhs, and would have been inappropriate—like calling a restaurant Mohammed or Krishna and serving pork and beef.)

At the time, Meeru and I were newly separated. It wasn't clear where our relationship was headed. Meeru, who is American, liked the idea of returning, part-time, to the U.S., and rented a condo in downtown Seattle.

I was her partner by default. But I had nothing to do with Shanik's operation: I went down for opening night, then twice more. That's it. We remained partners in Vij's and Rangoli, but now each of us was running our own side project under the Vij's umbrella. Mike, meanwhile, was preparing to launch Vij's Sutra, a curry bar, on his own in Victoria's old Hudson's Bay building.

Oğuz dealt with all front-of-house and financial issues at Shanik. Meeru's focus was strictly the kitchen, the food, and doing public cooking events. She hired new Americans to staff the kitchen, in this case immigrants from Ethiopia. She'd come to realize that Ethiopian cuisine uses similar spices and decided to shake things up. They spoke only Amharic. Some came from refugee camps.

She and Oğuz planned to rotate weeks. But nothing ran smoothly. Shanik was a headache from day one, and both were driving back and forth every week. To add more stress, Oğuz's marriage to Kari was falling apart, and would not survive.

Some initial letdown was inevitable. Vij's was known in Seattle, and not just among the food-obsessed who used to trek up the I-5 to eat there. Expectations were high. And Shanik's opening was about as bumpy as they come. Not only were there last-minute issues with key equipment, including the fridges and exhaust systems, but a few nights before opening, some of the kitchen staff informed Meeru that they couldn't work nights because there was no public transit to get them home to the suburban cities surrounding South Seattle. In the end, she was able to keep them by organizing a carpool. The local press pounced—for all the wrong reasons. Her food never suffered.

It got so stressful that Meeru avoided drinking water at night: Midnight bathroom trips would end with her lying awake, worrying. Amazon staff were demanding discounts on the food and a $6.99 buffet. But Meeru was unwilling to bend: At fifty, she wasn't about to start selling cheap, antibiotic-laden chicken just to make a buck. Meeru and I are not fast-food people.

The dining room, designed by Heliotrope Architects, a local Seattle firm, was bright, elegant, and comfortable. But one reviewer wrote that it had the feel of a condo's ground floor. And I wasn't there circling the room, greeting everyone. The menu was inventive. Vegetarians were especially happy. But reviews were mixed, with some unfairly comparing the cuisine at Shanik to Vij's, a different restaurant with a separate menu, price point, and cost structure. Meeru felt about Shanik's opening as I had about Rangoli's. To her, Shanik was being overshadowed by its well-known older sibling.

After opening with a no reservations policy, Meeru and Oğuz were forced to bring one in. There was no way someone would risk driving an hour and a half in Seattle traffic without knowing whether they'd get a table. They reworked their first attempt at a takeout counter, offering inexpensive chicken and chickpea curries served with a sprouted lentil salad and rice for quick lunches. She had to consider what her customers were demanding.

By the end, they were serving two very different demographics: daytime customers wanting a quick bite and evening guests who wanted an intricate meal and ambiance. What a brutal, confusing model.

Meeru had always believed that Vij's could be successful anywhere in the world. She learned the hard way that this is not necessarily true. She'd wanted to build a Rangoli, an Indian bistro. But her partners wanted a Vij's, a destination restaurant. Rangoli would have worked. Vij's did not. They were packed on Friday and Saturday nights, but weeknights were brutal. And this was no Yaletown: South Lake Union was a ghost town after five p.m.

Seattle is a city of neighbourhoods, and people tend to stick close to home.

Oğuz initiated the conversation about pulling out. He explained to Meeru how Shanik was doing, how long it could survive if nothing changed. She trusts his judgment innately, and ultimately understood. Her saving grace was this: In the final month, after announcing Shanik's closing, the restaurant saw the same two-hour lineups as Vij's every night. And on its last evening, Meeru dined with the head of real estate of Amazon and Vulcan. They drank champagne; their good intentions shone through. For Meeru and Oğuz, this ending was crucial to returning home with confidence. Most importantly—for the girls and me—Meeru stopped whining about moving back to the States and began loving Vancouver in earnest.

Meeru is still conflicted. It was the hardest thing she'd ever worked for in her life. She hadn't even known she had the strength in her. But three years later, what did she have to show for it? Taking inventory really hurt. She'd lost me. She'd lost Shanik. It was a dark time. I was devastated for her. But we kept our heads held high.

Through it, she became a whip-smart businessperson. She and Oğuz learned, the hard way, what not to do with a restaurant business. In this industry, location really is everything. They're currently planning a new Turkish-Indian venture on Vancouver's Granville Street.

Meeru thinks I'm just like her dad. He's a bit old world, so we get along like a house on fire. But I think Meeru is his double. She just doesn't realize it. She has the same refugee's tenacity, a resilience to fight and survive. That's why she's still standing today. But it also causes her problems. It pushes her into fights she doesn't need to engage in. It causes her to feel cornered when she's not. She even drives like her dad! She doesn't realize any of this, and I tend to avoid telling her. Theirs is not an easy relationship.

But Meeru will say that the best thing that came of Shanik was the way it allowed me to rekindle my relationship with our daughters, which had fractured in the aftermath of the separation. They couldn't understand what had happened and, seeing me move out, had sided with their mom, thinking that I was in the wrong. That I hadn't considered their feelings, thinking only of myself.

The first nine months of 2012 had been tumultuous: I'd see them every Sunday for dinner, although they didn't want to spend time in my condo (I didn't blame them—I can barely stand the place). But with Meeru in Seattle, I became the primary parent. That's when I got my parenting groove back.

Initially, Meeru went to Seattle for three months, with only weekend trips back home. So the girls went from having very little of Papa in their lives to having me every single day. I still remember when Meeru first returned after being gone an entire month. She was coming in late on a Saturday night after closing Shanik. In my efforts to keep the girls awake to greet their mother I put on *The Shawshank Redemption*, a favourite movie of mine. Previously the girls would have gotten angry at my selfishness. This time, they laughed at the "dorky" choice. I knew things were improving. Meeru will tell you that this is when she rekindled her faith in me as a father. And the weird energy that had sat over the house for almost a year began dissipating.

I would plan elaborate breakfasts for them. Every morning I'd have the BBC on when they came downstairs, and hand them a fresh-squeezed juice. I took it all very seriously. Before going to work I'd cook dinner, then be home by four p.m. to reheat it for them, setting the dinner table with candles. Or I'd leave a pot of chickpeas on the stove for a snack and then come home to cook a surprise—mac and cheese with cauliflower, or Spätzle, a creamy, baked German pasta. I'd be home again after the dinner shift by nine-thirty to make sure they got to bed on time.

At first they were angry with me. I knew I couldn't reason with them. I couldn't fight with them. All I could do was be patient, swallow their hurtful comments, accept their anger. Their pain was legitimate.

I needed to win back their love and trust. I did it, gently, through humour and food.

I don't have an easy time expressing emotions, feelings. But through food, I can love you. I can be generous with you. You're crying—I can fix you. I can cheer you up. To this day, my biggest thrill comes in hearing one of my daughters say "Papa—this is so delicious," her voice full of excitement. I live for their praise. There have been times when they've brought tears to my eyes.

I make simple, delicious meals for them: Baked potato with cream and cheese and chives—things I know they love. I'll start thinking about it a day or two in advance, picking up fish they might like, French lentils, heavy cream, worrying about whether they'll like this or that ingredient, fussing endlessly over the menu. Presentation is important to me, so we'll pretend to be eating in a restaurant. Shanik used to like to test me, asking for falafel schnitzel or fried strudel just to see whether I could pull it off. Invariably, I did.

In a sense, I suppose I cooked my way back into their hearts. Had Meeru not gone to Seattle I might never have had the chance to get to know the girls in this way. That's also when Meeru and

I stopped fighting. I remember once, on her drive to Seattle, she stopped at My Shanti and had a drink with me; we had a fabulous time, and she kissed me in front of the staff and said "I love you."

It's so bizarre. Sometimes I look at her and think, You're the love of my life, and I know in my heart that one day we'll be together again. And other times I'll think, Thank God we're not together anymore.

Every so often I'll ask Ashwin whether we should have broken up with our wives. "But we did," he'll always say. "And here we are now." It's taken years, but both of us now have healthy, solid relationships with our ex-wives. "We'll be bound to those women by our daughters for the rest of our lives," Ashwin will add. "It's imperative, for our girls' sakes, that we keep that relationship strong."

"Come," he always says. "Let's go live this life while we still can."

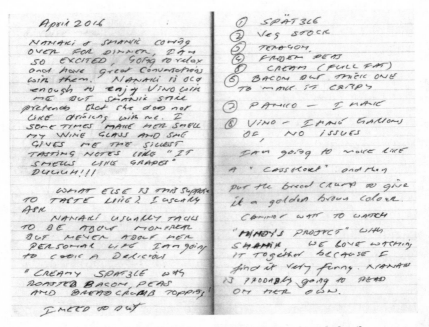

My journal notes planning dinner and an evening with Nanaki and Shanik.

I chose the restaurant business. I work passionately at it, and I love my life.

Five by Fifty

IN THE END, I DID MANAGE TO LAUNCH five major projects by fifty—but by the skin of my teeth. The fifth and final project, the new Vij's on Cambie Street, our signature restaurant, opened shortly before my fifty-first birthday, in December 2015—after delay upon delay.

I quietly toasted this small victory alone, with a bottle of champagne. We're not yet out of the financial rut, so I'm not celebrating yet. But I did want to mark the occasion. I'd done it: We had five major businesses, all under the Vij's banner. I shed more than a few tears thinking back to all the hardships, all that was lost in getting here.

We'd bought the space in 2007. Meeru and I used to walk past the unusually long, skinny red-brick building on our way from home to work at Vij's on 11th Avenue. "We should buy that building," I used to always say. It's a full city block long: From a visibility standpoint, you can't get any better. Then one day a "For Sale" sign appeared on an outer wall. I immediately phoned my lawyer and put in an offer for $1.57 million. The owner countered at $1.7 million. I signed a cheque for the deposit that very day.

I'd always wanted to buy in Cambie Village, as the south Cambie neighbourhood is known. I'm Indian: We love owning property, and I knew the investment would pay dividends. The Canada Line—Translink's third major SkyTrain line, connecting Richmond and the Vancouver International Airport with the downtown core—was then being built beneath Cambie Street, a busy north–south corridor.

With the space, I wanted to create our lantern-lit Taj Mahal. But at every step, it seemed, I hit a roadblock. Even inking the deal was a nightmare. The owner cashed my cheque for $20,000, then refused to sign the land title over to me. She'd panicked, realizing she'd made a mistake, and wanted more money before closing the deal. (We had to put a lien on the building and sue to close.)

She'd been renting the space for $7000 a month to a Thai immigrant running a Chinese restaurant. The poor guy was barely making ends meet. For two years I let him stay, even though making rent every month seemed next to impossible. "Tomorrow, sir—tomorrow, I promise" was all I ever heard from him. I was always after him for it.

Letting him stay was a mistake. After falling $40,000 in arrears, he packed up his family and vanished in the middle of the night. And when I busted down the door the next day, I couldn't believe Vancouver Coastal Health had been letting them serve food.

The kitchen was coated in a thick layer of grease. There were mouse droppings everywhere. The woks were dirty as hell; clearly, they were never washed. A small pond of dark, brackish water occupied the centre of the kitchen, where water dripping from the fridges had pooled. A makeshift bridge made of two-by-fours was the only way to cross.

I wasn't going to bother to take legal action—even if I successfully sued, I'd never be able to collect. The family was in rough shape. The kids had been sleeping in bunks above the kitchen. I'm not the type to kick a man when he's down. And I believe in karma and kismet—destiny, or fate. He'll get his comeuppance, just as I'll earn back the money lost.

But I was also to blame for delays in getting the new, signature Vij's off the ground. In 2008, less than a year after buying the Cambie site, I bought the property in Cloverdale for the factory. That's when our financial stresses truly began to bite. Vij's and Rangoli had to carry the financial weight of both the factory and the Cambie Street construction projects. It was like having one income supporting multiple families.

We were strapped, particularly when we broke ground on Cambie in 2014.

Marc tried to build on the theme of the first restaurant: the lanterns. Because the building itself is so big, so odd, we unified the exterior with a giant pink steel screen. It filters the lights of the city, creating a lantern-like effect—and a bit of a sound barrier. Cambie is a busy, noisy thoroughfare.

I've never wanted a massive, 250-seat restaurant. I've always wanted to be able to walk the whole floor, be able to touch every table, greet everyone who comes in. The personal touch, I believe, is the genius behind my restaurants and the reason for my success.

And that's not easy to replicate in such a huge space. I can't be in more than one place at once. At Rangoli, people don't expect to see me—it's Meeru's domain. But at My Shanti, at Vij's, they do. Everything hinges on it. From my earliest days, from the little fourteen-seat restaurant on Broadway on, that's been my focus. Twenty years later, the first thing people get when they arrive at the restaurant is a cup of chai.

To me, the restaurant is an extension of my home: When I welcome people to my home, I greet them at the door. I offer them food, drinks. I say goodbye as they're leaving. The strength of any strategy lies in its simplicity. Complexity tends to paralyze.

Our model of service—subtle, unobtrusive, with an obsessive eye to detail—is modelled after the European system. But I've added some more democratic, new-world variations. Our guests are treated regally, but equally. I firmly believe that they should all be treated with the same amount of love and respect regardless of caste, creed, or wealth.

And I have just one rule for myself, for my servers: No alcohol until the end of service. I won't take a sip until all the work is done. That's when I'll ask Mike to mix me a drink. I knock it back fast, often in a single swallow. I like that initial buzz as the alcohol jolts my system, and I allow myself to relax, to calm down after a long night.

I don't live a normal life. I never will. I can't go to dinner parties. I can't go to concerts. With the exception of Sundays, all my nights are spent in our restaurants.

I don't go to sleep until well after midnight. Before I do, I always smoke a cigarette—one of two I allow myself per day. I'm an insomniac. Meeru is always on my case to read, too, even for ten minutes, to calm my mind. If anyone needs to do that, it's me.

My days are long. They begin between five and six a.m., when

I start replying to emails, texts, and calls. The kitchen at Rangoli opens at six a.m. That's when chefs begin prepping the evening meal. Vij's is humming by six-thirty in the morning. My days are fully booked with back-to-back meetings.

My only break comes at two forty-five p.m., when I take a forty-five-minute nap. That's how I recharge. Because I work until nine or ten every night, I couldn't survive without it. I'm awake by three forty-five, showering and getting ready for the five-thirty hard open, when most people are calling it quits for the day. Right now, I'm spending three nights a week at My Shanti and three nights at the new Vij's on Cambie. Sunday night, as always, I'm home with Meeru, Shanik, and Nanaki, when she's home from McGill.

But I have no complaints about my life. And none of this feels like a sacrifice. I chose this business. I work passionately at it, and I love my life. I feel nothing but fortunate to be able to do what I love.

When we opened the new Vij's flagship on Cambie, we brought in Jay Jones, widely considered Vancouver's top bartender, to grow our cocktail program. In 2012 he was GQ's "most imaginative bartender" and enRoute magazine's Canadian Bartender of the Year. We've hired a second sommelier on the floor to help Mike with buying and sourcing—to try to find fun, unique wines and build to a 150-bottle list. We want to cap it there. We still have a $39 bottle, and our most expensive wine right now tops out at $250.

This summer, we launched a rooftop bar where we sell drinks and appetizers. Lights filter up to it from the dining room. From the street you'll see the lights from the roof on down, and the lantern effect has finally taken shape.

From the rooftop you can see the house where we raised our daughters. I climb up there every night, when I finish up at the restaurant, to dream up ways to turn My Shanti and the factory around. Although I don't dwell on my sorrows in public, I sometimes feel like a circus clown who makes everyone laugh but is crying inside.

The stress I've brought upon my family and my staff weighs on me. Once we reach our first year of profitability at the Cloverdale factory, I've promised to share the earnings equally with our core staff, all of whom have worked so selflessly to build the business.

My life at home has also changed dramatically. Shanik, now seventeen and in her last year of high school in Vancouver, is exactly like me: more fiery-tempered than her older sister, more quick to anger. She's witty, always at ease, ready to find the humour in any given situation. And sometimes we butt heads. That's not a bad thing; it's healthy, especially since I've learned to sit back and hear her out.

Shanik is strong, deeply protective of her mother. Her mom and I recently fought, and when Meeru asked me to leave and I hung back a second, Shanik stepped in: "Mama is telling you to go," she gently scolded me. "You have to leave now." I'm the same way with my mother. I like that about her.

Both girls attended neighbourhood French immersion schools. Meeru and I strongly believe in the Canadian public school system. We never wanted to privately educate them.

Nanaki is now nineteen and studying environmental science at McGill University in Montreal; she's confident and extremely articulate. She's Meeru's twin—the reason the two of them will sometimes lock horns. She's serious, sensitive, and analytical. My relationship with her has changed dramatically over the past three years.

The separation had left her hurt and upset. For a year, she barely spoke to me. Then one night, when she was seventeen, she came home drunk after a night at Trout Lake, a park in East Vancouver. Meeru was furious, and called me over.

"I can't even afford to go to Starbucks to buy coffee with my friends," Nanaki complained through tears. It was ridiculous. Of course we can afford Starbucks. But too much was changing, and too quickly.

The next morning, Shanik and Meeru drove to Bellingham, just across the U.S. border, to have lunch, leaving Nanaki and me together. For three hours, Nanaki laid into me. In her angriest moment, she told me she liked her mom better than me. She meant none of it, she'll tell you today.

But it helped our relationship enormously. Her anger with me began to dissipate once she was able to tell me what had been bothering her. Over time, Nanaki has come to understand that even if she didn't think Papa was right, that's life. She's come to accept the family's new order. She's on her own in Montreal, at university, finding her way.

Last summer, she worked as a server at Rangoli earning $9000 over four months, enough to cover her tuition at McGill. I think it showed her how hard we've had to work to create this life for our family. I was so proud of her. I'm able to see her one on one when I'm in Montreal, in Toronto; we interact as equals now, as adults, an incredible new phase in our relationship where we can speak openly and freely. Often, she'll join me at the bar at Vij's for a chat.

I recently began planning a trip to India. Nanaki told me she'd like to accompany me. "Really?" I practically shouted, unable to conceal my excitement. When I was finally alone in my hotel room that night I cried; I was so moved. Growing up, Nanaki and Shanik wanted nothing to do with India: the food, the culture, the music. All of it they disdained.

When they were little, I always wanted them to learn about their heritage, their culture, but Meeru saw things differently. When I'd raise the idea of weekend Indian dance classes or Hindi lessons, Meeru would push back: "Let them sleep in!" When I tried to play Indian music or Bollywood movies, the girls would follow their mother's lead and shut them off.

We're not preparing them to enter the restaurant business. Meeru is very firm on this: She wants them to do as they please in life. If it were up to me I would have had them in the restaurants from an earlier age, learning the ropes, to instill a strong work ethic. From the time I was a boy my father forced me to spend a few hours in his shop every afternoon, and I'm thankful for it. I can't help thinking I've done my daughters wrong in not instilling similar lessons in them.

After Nanaki left for McGill, I was emotionally blindsided: Her absence undid me. I felt like my heart was breaking. Soon after, I got a tattoo for the girls on my left wrist.

The image I chose for the tattoo, a silhouette inked in black, came from a photo Meeru took years ago of the two girls playing in a tidal pool on a South African beach; they were six and eight at the time. I can't remember ever feeling as happy as I did on that trip. I can still see them, their dark curls, their bright pink and orange bathing suits. I remember the feel of their tiny, sticky fingers in my hand, their near-weightlessness in my arms—all skinny arms and legs. Even if I don't see them as often, now that I'm living in the condo, the tattoo allows me to kiss them every morning before I begin my day.

Devoting myself to building up my five businesses fills me with the same energy and excitement I felt when Papa and I launched Vij's on Broadway.

BRAND GROWTH

FROM HERE ON OUT, the bulk of our projects will follow the royalty model: We don't want to spend any more money opening anything new. My five major projects are up and running; I want to spend the next ten years nurturing them, growing them. And frankly, my hands are tied. For the time being the banks won't lend me any more money unless I want to bring on a strategic partner. Meeru and I recently sold our house, not for financial reasons but because the home was too big for just Meeru. Nanaki is at McGill, and Shanik is leaving for university in 2017. Meeru bought a beautiful condominium with her half; mine went to servicing my debts.

But if we love an idea, if the project is fun and interesting and we feel confident in its long-term success, we'll agree to enter a partnership and lend the Vij's name through a licensing agreement. In the food industry, our name has come to signal quality.

In 2014, for example, I collaborated with Neal Brothers Foods to make spicy, masala-flavoured potato chips—Vij's Delhi-Licious chips. In 2016, capitalizing on the interest in craft beer, My Shanti launched a blond lager made of coriander and orange peels. At Vij's, we launched our Rajastan Red, in partnership with Oliver, B.C.'s Desert Hills Estate Winery. To celebrate our relocation to Cambie Street in 2015, we created a craft gin, Vij's Bolly Water. Gin is every bartender's go-to spirit, the linchpin of many drinks. And gin and tonic is as Indian as Gandhiji. Ours is a classic London dry–style savoury gin, with notes of coriander, ginger, and fennel meant to complement our Indian fare.

I should feel on top of the world right now. We have multiple major deals in the pipeline. After five years of headaches, the factory recently broke even in back-to-back months. The first quarter of 2016 looks like our best yet. Numbers are up at Rangoli. Reviews for the newly opened Vij's—my fifth and final project on Cambie Street— have been excellent, without exception. The new team at Vij's is working well, and the transition to the new space was flawless.

The prime minister's team recently called to arrange a private dinner at Vij's for Justin Trudeau, the thirteen premiers, and three Indigenous leaders, who were meeting in Vancouver for a First Ministers' conference, the first in over a decade. I hung up feeling elated. And yet the following day, I had a meeting with the land-lord at Morgan Crossing, Strathallen Capital Corp., to ask for a $5000 rent rebate until business at the new development picks up. Right now it's too steep, I argued.

One minute I'm fielding a call from the prime minister's team, and the next I'm begging for rent relief for My Shanti. None of this is unusual when you're juggling different businesses in different phases. It's like riding a rollercoaster I can't get off: One minute I'm climbing and the next I come crashing down.

What truly suffers is my time with Nanaki and Shanik. Between my busy schedule and their social lives, it's hard to find time for them. And when I see them I'm irritable, short. "Why are you being so rude, and not fun?" Shanik recently asked. It was a fair question. The answer is that I'm on the cusp of regaining our recent losses, and I can't be distracted. I need to dig in my heels and pull us through it. But it also feels like all systems are go and there's nothing more I can do; there are no more businesses left to open.

The other night I dreamed I was at the Kennedy Space Center in Cape Canaveral. I was at the launch complex, sitting alone in a rocket, all suited up, the clock counting down: five, four, three, two, one. But nothing happened. All around me the engines were revving, clouds of smoke billowing upward. But I was still grounded. I kept looking around, trying to figure it out: Why am I not lifting off? That's what my life feels like right now: that all systems are go, but I can't take off. The dream shook me. I sat alone in my empty glass condo, drinking a glass of water at three a.m. I never did get back to sleep.

I know what the dream meant. I am ready for takeoff. The right people and teams are in place at every location. Our food is perfect. Each space is dazzling and unique. Awards and new accolades continue to pour in. Everything is lined up. All that's missing is patience from me.

After a decade spent exhaustively creating and building my empire, finding and conceiving of five separate ventures, all constructed from the ground up, I need to learn to change gears, to sit back, to allow time for money to accumulate so that we have enough of a cushion that I can begin repaying our debts and we can all breathe again.

I can feel it coming. It began with the new year. I've entered a new phase; it's a rebirth, of sorts.

Devoting myself to building up my five businesses fills me with the same energy and excitement I felt when Papa and I launched Vij's on Broadway more than two decades ago, back when Mama was lugging curries in from Richmond. Meeru and I were holding hands back then, deeply in love. We're arm in arm these days, the best of friends. Back then we'd begun discussing adoption. Just this morning, we smiled at each other as we watched our beautiful daughters share a joke at our expense (Nanaki and Shanik were mimicking the way Meeru and I dance).

As I learn to live with small frustrations I keep thinking of a fable my grandmother used to tell me, about an elephant king who ruled over the jungle like a cruel despot. All the other animals were terrified of him. He'd reach his tusk down and pick up smaller animals, hurtling them up above the canopy just to show his dominance.

Then one day the animals banded together to try to figure out what to do. A small monkey volunteered to take him on. While the elephant was napping the monkey embedded a tiny sliver into the elephant's trunk. It was a constant irritant—it drove the poor animal bananas. He kept rubbing his trunk and sneezing, trying to get rid of it. He grew exhausted, and lay down. He was spent. He couldn't even get up to feed himself. In the end, the monkey spared him, removing the sliver.

The moral is twofold: It's not only the big things in life that can tear you down, and the king of the jungle is no less vulnerable to a tiny sliver than the smallest animal. Right now, My Shanti is my sliver.

But I know that's just temporary. A few months ago, it was the factory. And before that, it was Rangoli. The inner emotional stress, the headaches, the upheaval—it's all part of being an entrepreneur. It's the flip side of success, the part we don't normally air, the stuff we withhold from interviews, from media. But with this book I wanted to share with you the whole truth: the love, the glory, and the heartache.

Focus on the love and glory. Trust me, it makes the rest so worthwhile.

EPILOGUE

I almost didn't make my dinner with Trudeau. The First Ministers' dinner was slated for Wednesday, March 2. I'd had to fly to Toronto to speak at Restaurants Canada's annual spring trade show, and was scheduled to fly home to Vancouver on Tuesday.

That snowy Tuesday morning, on my way to give my remarks at the Enercare Centre, I got a text from the office saying that Toronto's Pearson Airport had begun cancelling flights because of a brewing blizzard. I panicked.

I got through my speech as quickly as I could. Nanaki was there with me; we'd had plans to spend the day together, catching up with industry types I rarely get a chance to see. I told her I had to catch a cab, and asked her to work the room on our behalf. Then, once I'd reached my hotel, I asked the cabbie to let the meter run—I didn't want to risk losing it while I ran upstairs and hurriedly packed.

The snow was coming down hard by the time I got to the airport, around eleven, and there was a long line of people trying to fly out. At one point I caught a glimpse of the monitor, which just read "CANCELLED . . . CANCELLED . . . CANCELLED . . . "

There wasn't a single seat left on any of the afternoon flights to Vancouver. By four-fifteen, after three failed standby attempts, I'd sweated through my shirt. The last afternoon flight was fully booked, and then a miracle: One spot had opened, and my name was called. I could have cried from relief. I'd spent the previous six hours gripped with anxiety. When I got home that night, I poured myself a large scotch—three fingers, or more. I put a cube of ice in the glass and then drained it in one sip, feeling it tear at my throat as it burned its way down. I could feel the alcohol entering my bloodstream, engulfing me all at once. Then I passed out.

I woke at two a.m., famished. I hadn't eaten all day. In the freezer I had a naan dough ball. I proofed it for a half-hour, then pounded it, making a pizza with fresh tomatoes, hot sauce, and Indian pickles before returning to bed.

The next day, we covered the tables at Vij's with candles and colourful, strikingly beautiful saris. I'd had five buckets of fresh rose petals delivered and covered the floor with them. Security and police officers were crawling all over the place. I kept getting updates from the Prime Minister's Office: "He's in the motorcade," then "He's ten minutes away," then finally, "He's two minutes out." I was greeting Ontario premier Kathleen Wynne, who came dressed in a stunning red jacket, and B.C.'s Christy Clark; they were the first to arrive. I had to awkwardly abandon them—"Just a minute, Kathleen," I said, running out the door.

As the prime minister's motorcade pulled up outside, I was standing in a Namaste, my head solemnly bowed, my palms pressed together at my heart, my fingers pointing skyward, my thumbs

tight against my chest. I was bowing to the divine in him, according to the Hindu tradition.

Justin Trudeau gripped me in a tight hug, like an old friend. I
have known him since he was a young Vancouver teacher.

People had lined up on the sidewalk. "Justin, we love you!"
they shouted. The prime minister called out my kitchen staff and
took selfies with each one. Whether he does good things for the
country, only time will tell. But he is a kind man.

The night opened with a poem performed by two First Nations
girls. Then Justin spoke, telling the premiers why he believes Vij's is
one of the world's best Indian restaurants. When he really wanted to
impress a girl (way before he got married), he said, he'd bring her here.
I remember him coming in after his brother Michel, then twenty-
three, was killed in an avalanche in Kokanee Glacier Provincial Park.
He'd brought his father, both of them sombre, ashen-faced.

Meeru managed to crack up the prime minister at the dinner
when he asked for the story behind the lamb Popsicles: "It's very easy
to please a white man with cream, garlic, and red meat," she joked.

I served the prime minister and the premiers myself, spooning
beef short ribs and rice onto their plates. My back was killing me by
the end of the night. Saskatchewan premier Brad Wall—tickled to
learn that our plates are Regina-made—talked up the province's
chickpea industry. Saskatchewan produces almost two-thirds of the
world's yield, including a majority of what India consumes.

By ten p.m. they'd left, twenty of the most important people
in Canada. I grabbed a drink, not to contemplate things but to gulp
down as I made for the front door.

Outside, the rain was coming down hard—unusually hard for
Vancouver. For months and months, the rains rarely relent. But

they're delivered in mists, gently, unobtrusively, and this felt more like Bombay during monsoon season. The sidewalk was being lashed in sheets. God, I miss the violence of the rains of my childhood.

I stood in the deluge, my back to the street, staring up at the neon purple sign bearing my grandfather's name, Papa's name, and mine. I let the rains pound my shoulders and soak through my clothes, cleansing me. What a trip the night had been.

That high took me back to my earliest days in the kitchen. I thought of Austria, of the plucky line chef I was, with my broken German and wrong-coloured skin, trying to impress my masters with salad. None would have believed what was inside me—the passion, the will, and the ambition. Their abuse steeled me, readying me for the hard years that followed. None of this has been easy. Not a single day. But my God, what a journey it has been.

EIGHT KEY LESSONS
I LEARNED IN LIFE

1. BE YOURSELF

Understand yourself. If you need to, spend some time getting comfortable with who and what you are. Then stand up for it—the good, the bad, and the ugly.

Never hide from what you are, from your history. I'm overweight. I'm an immigrant. I'm a college dropout. I've been married twice. I'm all these things. They reflect the life I have lived. I'm proud of it all.

And anyway, whatever you try to hide or deny will find you. I tried once to be thin. It didn't work. It's not me. I love good food and wine too much. The weight came right back.

2. DO YOUR HOMEWORK

Any time I give a talk or a presentation or go into a meeting—even if it's a quick, casual coffee with a longtime associate—I'm prepared. I've thought ahead about what I need to say, and written it down. Throughout the day, I take copious notes in a book I always carry with me.

Never think you can wing it. You can't.

Draw up an outline before every meeting. Come up with a process—how you plan to achieve what you've set out to do. Memorize your plan. Then follow it through.

3. KEEP YOUR KITCHEN IMMACULATE

A kitchen is a reflection of who you are. You can hide in your own home, be a pig in your car. But your kitchen, or office—that's your public face.

It reflects you. It sends a message out to the world. Are you organized? Conscientious? Efficient? That's how you want people to see you.

Consider your kitchen, or your office, as your mirror.

And if you work in a kitchen, never stand around waiting for something to do. Tidy up. Wipe the stainless steel fridge. Polish the sink. Take pride in your workplace, and show your employer who you really are, how much you care.

4. STAY ON TOP OF YOUR GAME

Once you reach the top, you can't coast.

Whether your aim is to create a Michelin-starred restaurant or run a successful business, getting there means taking nothing for granted, and constantly taking on new challenges.

I agreed to appear on *Dragons' Den* just two years into my TV career. I learned everything there is to know about craft beer. I took a sommelier course. I constantly visit other restaurants to try to figure out what the competition is doing better, what the next food trend might be.

I take a forty-five-minute nap every afternoon. This allows me to stay on top of my game from six a.m. to ten p.m., six days a week. Figure out your equivalent of a nap. (Not caffeine.) Use it to recharge.

Great chefs know everything there is to know about making a restaurant successful. That requires constant upkeep.

5. RESULTS ARE ALL THAT MATTER

In the end, what the customer thinks of the product is all that counts. Period.

You may think you've created the most brilliant dish, but if customers don't like it, you've failed. See it for what it is: a flop. Scrap it, and forget it.

The only thing that matters is that a customer walks away thinking, That's the best meal I've ever had. That's how you hook them. That's when they keep coming back.

6. EMBRACE SIMPLICITY

This has been the hardest lesson for me. Once I was able to buy expensive clothes, live in a beautiful home in central Vancouver, and drink expensive wines, it became hard to embrace simplicity when business decisions required it of me.

But rather than feeling depressed, or pining for what I once had, I embraced it.

Live simply but proudly. Even if you can't afford expensive shoes, be proud of the pair you do have. Take pride in who you are becoming. And accept what is necessary on the road there.

7. NEVER FORGET A CUSTOMER

As a teenager, I was forced to watch my father at work in his shop in Bombay after school every day. At the time I hated it. I was so bored.

But as I watched my father wheeling and dealing, I noticed that he remembered his past customers. Always. And I'd watch their faces light up with a wide smile whenever he did, a familiarity that helped grease the sale.

It taught me a valuable lesson: There's no sound in life sweeter than your own name. Remembering a customer is one of the most important things you can do in the restaurant industry.

8. LEARN FROM YOUR FAILURES

Failure is how we learn and grow. Failure shows us what needs correcting. Failure teaches us to stay humble. Embrace it. From success, we learn nothing.

When you make a mistake, do what you need to fix it. Own up to it, and don't dwell.

Great chefs take the hit, suck it up, then go out and do better the next time. After all, there will always be another meal. Another deal. Another opportunity.